A PROACTIVE APPROACH

FAITHfully
Parenting
PRESCHOOLERS

JOHN R. BUCKA

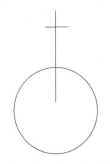

CONCORDIA PUBLISHING HOUSE · SAINT LOUIS

Library of Congress Cataloging-in-Publication Data

Bucka, John R., 1949-
　　Faithfully parenting preschoolers : a proactive approach / John R. Bucka.
　　　　p. cm.
　　ISBN 0-7586-0055-0
1. Parenting—Religious aspects—Christianity. 2. Preschool children—Religious life. 3. Parent and child—
Religious aspects——Christianity.
I. Title.
　　BV4529 .B836 2003
　　248.8'45—dc21　　　　　　　　　　　　　2002155453

1　2　3　4　5　6　7　8　9　10　　　　12　11　10　09　08　07　06　05　04　03

I dedicate this book to the countless parents of wonderful preschoolers as well as their children that I have met throughout my parish ministry. I have found that the more parents have shared with one another in their parenting journey, the more they have discovered the richness of God's power and love.

I write this book in honor of my wife Lynn, and my children,

Katherine,

Matthew,

Peter,

Jennifer,

Sarah,

and Kaaren.

They have contributed to my faith journey and the realization that life itself, and the relationships with the people that I love, are God's gifts. I am truly blessed by their love, patience, and support, and am forever grateful to God for the life we share.

Contents

Behavioral Ups and Downs

Assorted Cares and Concerns

Introduction

It is amazing isn't it? The one vocation that is a lifetime commitment—the calling to be a parent—comes with no training or previously acquired experience, especially for those who bring their firstborn home from the hospital or newly adopt. With each passing day, all the ideas that we had about parenting newborns, toddlers, or preschoolers seem to fly further out the window. Still, God calls us to raise our children to be good and love others; to respect authorities and be good citizens; to be good students and some day good spouses. The journey begins in the womb and accelerates at birth. These early years of parenting are joy-filled, anxiety-producing years.

What makes our calling as parents even more challenging is that it seems as if the world is changing each day, even each minute. Technology, concern for the enviroment, threats of terrorism, child abductions, changing morals and standards, and a fluctuating economy contribute to continual changes in our world. Despite our fears, however, what makes our calling bearable and even more rewarding is that as we begin our parenting journey, we remember that we are baptized parents. What hasn't changed is sin and its cure, forgiveness through Christ. Our children do not start their journey alone either. As we journey together, parents and children, our Lord and Savior, Jesus Christ, calls us into our vocations as moms and dads, sons and daughters. He calls us to repent and be forgiven daily within these vocations. It is in this baptized life that our children grow physically, mentally, and emotionally. They grow also in the faith that was planted in them in the waters of Baptism, when they were adopted into God's family in the name of Father, Son, and Holy Spirit.

FAITHfully Parenting Preschoolers: A Proactive Approach is rooted in God's Word and looks to God's Word as the source of guidance, direction, and hope for parents. God's Word directs us to two sources of help: our brain or common sense (reason) and His Word of repentance and forgiveness in the sacramental life. This book is based on the concept that we are members of a Christian parenting community that began with our own parents. God called us to care for, love, and support these precious gifts He has given us. Much of this book is just that, the wise use of the gifts of common sense. It is that community that we can learn from and give support to as our parenting journey continues.

Furthermore, we gain strength from our Lord as He gathers us to partake of His Holy Meal. We receive forgiveness from the body and blood of our risen Lord and Savior as He meets us in that meal and binds us together with Him, our Father in heaven, and with all believers. We receive hope from His sacramental presence, realizing that His grace is all we need. And, as we share His body and His blood, we know that His strength is perfect in the midst of our weaknesses.

FAITHfully Parenting Preschoolers does not have all the answers. But it does lead us to discover that our heavenly Father helps us find answers to questions that trouble us, with the help of His Word and the gift of the Christian community.

The Journey Begins . . .

Soon after our children arrive, we realize that we cannot undertake this journey alone. We need God's grace; we need direction from His Word; we need the help and support of friends and family. It is from His Word, the Ten Commandments, that we learn of our sin and repent. It is our Baptism that makes us children of our heavenly Father. It is that same Baptism that daily gives us grace and strength as we parent our preschoolers.

As we travel, we want to reach out to our fellow travelers as well as to other parents who have gone before us. It is said that it takes a village to raise a child; however, the reality of our world today is that all too often no one is home in the village. *FAITHfully Parenting Preschoolers* is an attempt to say to parents, "It is so important for your child and for yourself that you remain in the village." As members of the village that is the body of Christ, we not only support one another by sharing questions, solutions, and ideas we support one another by praying with and bringing forgiveness to one another. *FAITHfully Parenting Preschoolers,* then, provides hope and affirmation as we begin the wonderful, awesome journey of parenthood. Along the way, the Lord teaches us to rejoice in the gifts of heaven and in the gifts of the children God has given us.

Using This Book with Others As You Travel

If you use this book in a group setting, sessions could be held in a meeting room, classroom, or private home. Discussion leaders should be concerned first and foremost with the needs of the group and the direction in which the group wishes to travel. That means that if the group or an individual member of the group seems to have an overwhelming need to discuss a specific topic, such as television usage or separation anxiety, it is beneficial to begin with that section of the book. If after two sessions of dealing with childcare, for example, you seem to have exhausted the subject, then by all means move on.

A sample session may be organized in this way:

15 minutes: Check-in time. This is a time to discuss the joys and concerns, the highs and the lows of the group members' previous week. You might sense that a parent's highs or lows are significant enough for the group to spend more time dealing with one issue. If that is the case, say something like, "Mary, I sense this issue is really troubling you today. Before we continue, I wonder if we should spend some time with this. Does anyone have difficulty extending our discussion time and talking about this issue?" Then adjust the time you spend on other parts of the session or continue the session topic at the next meeting.

25 minutes: Dealing with the introduction, the case study, and the questions for discussion. The group leader or volunteers may read this material aloud.

30 minutes: Dealing with the **Parent Pairs** section. To facilitate group discussion, individuals should complete this section before the session.

5 minutes: Summary. Summarize the group discussion, then identify what the next session should cover, and close with prayer.

It is tempting for those of us who live in a postmodern world to place our own abilities to problem-solve or self-analyze over and above our need to continue to depend upon God's mercy and direction revealed in the absolute truth of His Word. Group leaders should listen carefully for opportunities to help group members center themselves on the Word of God; to encourage them to repent daily and enjoy their own baptismal mercy; to attend the Lord's Supper regularly; and to engage in family devotions and Bible study.

Some Final Words

Regardless of how you use this book, the primary purpose of *FAITHfully Parenting Preschoolers* is to lead you to God as the source of your strength and hope through the study of His Word, the sacramental life, and prayer. Each chapter provides thought-provoking questions to help you think through the many issues you will face as a parent. However, the most important questions will steer you to our heavenly Father and His will of mercy and forgiveness for every parent. There is our real freedom to parent our child and then pray: "Thy will be done." We are not alone; our Lord and Savior Jesus Christ provides for us as parents and as children—God's baptized and redeemed children.

I hope you will discover the joy of parenting and the privilege that God has given you as a parent. I also hope you will appreciate your preschooler for the precious person he or she is: a child of God who is daily growing, understanding, learning, and discovering the joy of God's creation and unconditional love. May God bless you, give you wisdom in your parenting, and grant you peace.

The author.

I prayed for this child, and the LORD
has granted me what I asked of Him.
So now I give him to the LORD. For his
whole life he will be given over to the LORD.
(1 Samuel 1:27–28)

The Issue of Day Care

Children truly are gifts that have been given to us by God. In some cases, they are the result of long and desperate prayers for the child to be conceived and to be born. In other cases, after long periods of waiting, the hoped-for child is received through the gift of adoption. We value our children as God's precious gifts, and because we do, we find it very difficult to choose who will care for them when we cannot be there. We search for people who are not only our representatives but God's representatives as well. We want caregivers who reflect our faith and reinforce the values we deem important for our children in order to grow to become God's faithful servants and enjoy His mercy.

Regardless of the circumstances—single parent or both mother and father working outside the home—the issue of day care is extremely important. How does a parent make an intelligent choice about day care? What are the characteristics of a good center or program? Does a parent place a child in private-home day care or the home of a relative? Does a parent choose a day care that is operated by a company or a corporation, or should the child be placed in a non-profit, church-based center? Does a parent invite a college student or a nanny into the home to become their provider?

These issues are vital, especially when it seems as if the child spends more time with the day care provider than with his parents. Parents need the wisdom of Solomon as they make choices about child care. It means that as Christian parents search, they need to look for day care providers who see their role as a service on behalf of the parents. They need to be confident that their day care providers will be partners in the child's care and upbringing and in continuing the journey of faith. When day care providers are servants and partners in the parenting process, that journey will continue to be a faithful one for parents as well as their children.

How can I know?

Shelly Brown gave birth to Cassandra a year ago. The corporation for which she works has a very open-ended maternity leave policy that guarantees Shelly job security for one year after the birth of her child. As she prepared to return to work, Shelly had decided to place Cassandra with the Kid's Place Day Care Center near their home.

Shelly was really not looking forward to returning to work, but her feelings were somewhat allayed because she was comfortable with her day care placement. That is until she ran into Julie and Sharon at a neighborhood coffee party. The conversation went something like this:

"Shelly, are you ready to get back into the rat race on Monday?" Julie asked.

"Not really, but at least I have my day care problem settled. I decided to place Cassie at Kid's Place Day Care Center. It's convenient and the director seems really nice," Shelly replied.

Sharon spoke up. "Shelly, I hate to disagree with you, but I tried Kid's Place when Jeffrey was younger. Whenever I picked him up from Kid's Place, he always seemed so hyper. Then, when he got home, he seemed bent on destroying everything in the house. This went on for about three weeks until I changed day care providers. I went from Kid's Place to a private provider. It made all the difference in the world. Jeffrey couldn't wait to go to day care every morning. And when I picked him up, he seemed like such a happy, contented kid. I hope you reconsider!"

Julie added, "I hate to tell you this, Shelly, but I had the same experience when my Carl went to Kid's Place!"

Shelly was confused and on the brink of tears. She said nothing.

What would you do?

- If you were Shelly, what would you do next?

- What are the features of a good day care program? What are your expectations? What do you want for your child?

- Although Sharon's and Julie's experiences with Kid's Place were not good, what might make Shelly's experience a different one?

- Sharon said she waited almost three weeks before changing day care providers. How long would you wait before changing your day care provider? On what basis would you make your decision?

- Sharon and Julie immediately voiced concerns about Shelly's choice of day care providers. What would make you voice the same concerns?

- What are the advantages of a corporate day care center over a private center? What are the advantages of a private center over a corporate one? What are the advantages of a church-based center? What are the advantages of a private home arrangement?

- If a child seems combative and destructive after a day care experience, what can parents do besides change providers? What questions would you ask a provider in such a situation?

- What would be your prayer for your day care provider and for your child as you enter this aspect of parenting?

Parents serve on behalf of God and our day care provider is our extension, our representative we have chosen to care for our child. Parents have great freedom and responsibility in making this decision based upon all the information we can gather. As we leave our child in someone else's hands, we trust that person will provide the love and care our child will want and need. But that necessary love and safekeeping go beyond even what the day care provider is able to give. As we leave our child in the care of someone else, we also trust that our Good Shepherd will provide the care and the love our child needs. Ultimately, we leave our child in His hands and pray, "Thy will be done."

You know your situation best, so before you decide upon day care arrangements, take time to decide what you need for your child and what you need for yourself as a parent.

- Do the provider's values and faith match yours?

- If the provider's faith is different, will they respect your faith?

- Is there adequate supervision and ample interaction among the children and between the adult(s) and children as well?

- Are there an acceptable number of adult caregivers for the number of children present?

- Does the provider seem to be a person who would build the self-esteem of your child?

- Does the provider let children watch television? If so, how much and what kind of programming. What videos does the provider show?

- Is there a scheduled quiet time or naptime?

- What schedule of payments does the provider require, especially during holidays or on sick days and for early drop-off or late pickup?

- Does the provider take scheduled field trips or provide for organized activities, such as swimming lessons?

- What kind of snacks does the provider offer?

- What is the provider's policy regarding bringing toys from home?

Those are only a few of the questions to consider as you look for suitable day care for your child. As you begin your search, ask your provider for references, people you can call and with whom you can discuss such topics. In addition, seek out people who have had experience with the day care provider you are considering or with day care providers in general. If their opinions are important to you, consider them as you come to a decision about your child's day care provider.

Finally, remember that no decision is cut in stone. God's Word does not reveal which daycare you should choose. You are free to choose. Pray for wisdom as you decide. Pray with your child about his or her day care experience. Pray for your day care providers as well, and let them know you are praying for them. And always assure your child that he will be well cared for and loved. That care and love are extensions of Jesus' love and God's grace. Trust that God's grace will surround your child and your caregiver at all times. For we live by God's grace. His grace covers us even when we make decisions that are not the best, that need to be re-evaluated, or that change. Sin is forgiven because of Christ's decision to suffer and die for it. It is God, in the end, who will continue to help our son or daughter grow in that grace and in that love for Him and for all people. Parents sin. Parents repent. Parents are forgiven. Get used to it. It is the way of daily life for the baptized parent.

Closing Prayer

Gracious God, thank You for the gift of children that You have put in my care on Your behalf. Help me as a parent to care for them and nurture them with the love You give them through Your Son and the care You provide through others. In Jesus' name. Amen.

Parent Pairs

How does a parent make the right decision about day care? What day care provides the best situation for our children so they not only grow in wisdom and stature, but they grow in their faith as well? How does God help and direct parents in the process of choosing a day care provider? Must Christian parents always place their children in a Christian day care?

Read 1 Samuel 1:27–28 and consider the following questions as you discuss the **Parent Pairs** section with your spouse or another parent.

The Issue of Day Care

(To be done with your spouse or another parent.)

1. Describe the day care environment you want for your child.

2. Describe the personality characteristics and the philosophy of the provider you believe are important for your child in order to have a positive day care experience.

3. List in order of importance what you want for your child as you place him or her in day care.

    ___ I want my child to grow in learning skills.

    ___ I want my child to learn about his or her baptized life in Christ.

    ___ I want the provider to reinforce my values and faith.

    ___ I want my child to have one-to-one quality time with a caring, loving adult.

    ___ I want my day care provider to have a firm but fair policy in setting limits for children.

    ___ I want day care to provide a variety of experiences for my child both inside and outside the day care facility, such as picnics, trips to the park, or other trips.

    ___ I am interested only in licensed day care centers.

    ___ I need to know that the staff/person can be trusted to care for my child in a loving way that builds his or her self-esteem.

    ___ I want my child in day care more than 20 hours a week.

4. List three day care providers within a reasonable distance from your home:

5. After evaluating day care providers, I have decided upon:

6. My prayer for my child as he enters day care is: *(You may write a prayer in this space.)*

7. My prayer for my day care provider as my child enters day care is: *(You may write a prayer in this space.)*

8. The best way for me to communicate to my child that God loves him while he is in day care and every minute of the day is: *(You may choose more than one answer.)*
   - ❏ Read Bible stories to my child at bedtime.
   - ❏ Say words like, "Remember, Sweetheart, Jesus loves you and so do I."
   - ❏ Teach songs and hymns like "Jesus Loves Me" or "To Your Temple Lord I Come."
   - ❏ Pray with my child.
   - ❏ Daily remind him of his Baptism.
   - ❏ Other.

9. I plan to evaluate my day care: *(Choose one.)*
   - ❏ Every month.
   - ❏ Every six months.
   - ❏ Every year.
   - ❏ I don't need to evaluate the day care; I just know things will be all right.

10. If things don't go well at day care, my plan would be:

11. If I had advice for friends who were looking for a day care provider, I would say:

12. The three most important questions to ask the references for my day care provider are:

13. If I were to be a reference for my day care provider to other parents, the three most important facts I would share would be:

14. The strength I draw upon from 1 Samuel 1:27–28 is:

When his parents saw Him, they were
astonished. His mother said to Him,
"Son, why have You treated us like this?
Your father and I have been anxiously
searching for You."
(Luke 2:48)

Trouble at the Day Care

It is typically the case that before we became parents, many of us had images of what our children would be like and what kind of parent we would be. In our pre-parent minds, we believed our children would be different from those of our friends or relatives. We thought our methods of discipline would be the most effective and we would minimize any harmful behavior that may rear its ugly head. Our children would always act as if they were God's gifts to us and to everyone else for that matter.

After we become parents, however, reality hits. There comes the time when our child behaves as though he is not God's gift to anyone. Sin rears its ugly head for us and our child. The romance of parenting is gone! When these times come, our child can frustrate us and test our patience. He fails to meet our expectations for good behavior or he acts out. When that behavior occurs in day care, we want to ask, as did Mary, "Child, why have you treated us like this?"

Of course, Jesus was sinless and, therefore, blameless. Mary was clearly in the wrong. However, we still ask the question. Then we remember our calling to be the parent. Our child isn't God, rather he is the sinner for whom God died. There will be times when our child will act out, vent his frustration and anger, and generally not be the kind of child we want him to be. Many times, such fits of anger happen in our homes; after all, home is a safe place for our child to express emotion. And when he does act out, it raises the question: What are normal expressions of frustration and how do we deal with them, especially the more harmful ones?

Our hope for our child at this early stage in life is that when he is away from us, in pre-school or day care, God will help him to know the difference between appropriate and harmful expressions of anger and frustration. Our prayer for our child at such times can be that God will keep him always as the apple of His eye, under the shadow of His almighty wing. As we give our little one into God's care whenever we leave him with others, we can trust our training to help him model behavior that pleases God. We pray that our child will reflect love the God gives through His Son, Jesus Christ, our Lord. We can trust that God's mercy and forgiveness will empower our child not only to mirror that love, but to share the forgiveness with others throughout the day by what he does and says.

He did what?

Aaron is a three-year-old boy who recently began going to Mrs. Carson's day care. For the first few weeks everything seemed wonderful, not only for Mrs. Carson but also for Aaron's father, Roberto. Each day when Roberto would come for Aaron, Mrs. Carson would tell him that Aaron was a very well-behaved little boy.

But one day when Roberto came to pick up Aaron after work, Mrs. Carson said to him, "Roberto, do you have some time? I want to tell you what Aaron did to Jake today."

Instantly concerned, Roberto sat and listened as Mrs. Carson told the following story:

"Jake and Aaron were playing together. Jake left Aaron to play with a toy tractor. When Jake did that, Aaron watched him for a while, then went over to him and took the tractor away. When Jake began to cry, Aaron bit him on the cheek. We're very happy that Jake wasn't seriously hurt. But I must say, Roberto, I'm very concerned that Aaron's behavior doesn't happen again. Will you please say something to him when you go home today?"

Startled, Roberto replied, "Why, yes, Mrs. Carson. I'll have a talk with Aaron, and I assure you nothing like this will ever happen again!"

Roberto did talk with Aaron, but two weeks later, Mrs. Carson called him into her living room and told him, "I'm sorry, Roberto, but nothing much has changed with Aaron's behavior. In fact, today he not only bit Jake, he threw something at him. I'm afraid I cannot tolerate this kind of behavior in my day care. You need to look for a new placement for Aaron."

What would you do?

- If you were Aaron's father, what more information would you need from Mrs. Carson before assessing this situation?

- If you were Mrs. Carson, what more information about Aaron would you need?

- If you were Jake's parent, what action would you expect Mrs. Carson to take that would prevent Aaron from biting again? How long would you want Mrs. Carson to tolerate the behavior before she asked Aaron to leave the day care?

- Aaron's father said he would have a talk with Aaron after the first incident. If you were Aaron's parent, what would you say to him?

- If you were Aaron's parent, what consequences would you give him for the continuing incidents?

- What consequences would you expect Mrs. Carson to give Aaron for biting and throwing?

- When your child has acted out, whether at day care or elsewhere, what were some of the helpful ways you chose to deal with the behavior? How did the behavior change? What were some ways that were not helpful?

- When you look at behavior such as Aaron's, what could be the cause of a child's biting or throwing, actions that seem on the surface to be unprovoked?

- What do you think Aaron needed from the day care provider and from his dad in this situation?

- How do three-year-olds deal with their frustrations, disappointments, and anger?

Parents are not always able to answer these questions so easily. We are tempted to impose our own set of rules and regulations before we try to understand what is behind the sometimes-inappropriate actions of our children.

Unacceptable behavior, like biting or throwing, can be the result of a child frustrated by his inability to communicate feelings. Sometimes, inappropriate behavior is an attempt to gain control over a situation in which they sense they have lost control. Children often resort to inappropriate behavior as a way of gaining the attention they need.

As parents, when we deal with our preschoolers we need to remember the two ways to handle them. Unacceptable or inappropriate actions are still wrong and sinful behavior. They are baptized children. We teach them to repent of their wrongdoing and we forgive them. Once we've dealt with them as **baptized** children, then we deal with them as baptized **children**. We teach them to do the right thing to be a good friend in preschool and a good child at home. Although we love the sinner, we never condone the sin. We can show that unconditional love to our children as we attempt to understand what is in their hearts and minds.

We need to listen to our children and assess what is causing the behavior. We are then better able to consider responses that not only help stop the undesirable behavior but reinforce that they are God's creations and forgiven. They are our precious children. Our response might be setting certain limits for our children, such as withdrawing a favorite television program or limiting other privileges. Or our response could be a system of behavior modification, such as rewarding them with "points" for good behavior at day care. Once our children achieve a certain number of points, we could reward them in a creative way that reinforces what we have taught about anger management and about showing love to others. Remember that each child may react differently to the same method of behavior reinforcement.

An additional response to wrong actions might be to add a nightly prayer that God would help them be good boys and girls when they go to their day care provider the next day. (Luther's evening prayer is a great one to teach them at bedtime.) We can also tell them that we will be praying for them during the day. We can let them know that when we pick them up, we want good reports from their caregivers. If we don't, there will be consequences for their bad behavior. Parents must follow through with those consequences. And we can let our children know how pleased we are when we hear that they are well behaved.

Whatever the case, it is good to remember that the word "discipline" comes from the word "disciple." As such, when we discipline our children, we are in every respect teaching them and reinforcing the knowledge within them that they are God's children, children of the heavenly Father, adopted into His family through Baptism into Christ. It is the same baptismal grace that our heavenly Father showers upon us that helps us develop our own style of reinforcing what we expect from our children.

We are not alone in our parenting. Our heavenly Father is with us every step of the journey, forgiving us and giving us strength to continue!

Closing Prayer

Heavenly Father, You know what it means to be a parent. You gave Your only Son to suffer and die for the sins of the world. Give me patience and understanding to deal with my child in a loving and kind way so I might share the forgiveness You have freely given me through Your Son, Jesus Christ, my Lord. Amen.

Parent Pairs

What can parents do about their child's inappropriate behavior? How can parents teach their child to deal with anger and frustration in positive ways? How can parents help children feel valued and precious and, at the same time, administer discipline in a way that reflects what God wants?

Read Luke 2:48 and consider the following questions as you discuss the **Parent Pairs** section with your spouse or with another parent.

Trouble at the Day Care

(To be done with your spouse or another parent.)

1. If I found out my child was acting out in a way that harmed other children at day care, I would:

   ☐ Become terribly upset with my child.

   ☐ Clarify what my child did that led to the incident.

   ☐ Try to find out more about the conditions of the day care and how my day care provider responds to the stress caused by those conditions.

   ☐ Try to examine what conditions in my child's environment at home or in the day care might be causing frustration.

   ☐ Try to determine my child's version of what happened.

   ☐ Reexamine the limits I set for my child and how effective they are.

   ☐ Be sure not to undermine the authority of the day care provider.

   ☐ Have my child apologize to the other child and to the teacher.

   ☐ All of the above.

   ☐ None of the above.

2. The one behavior I wish my child would change is:

3. In the past, three things I have tried to change the above behavior were:

4. One intervention that was helpful was:

5. The interventions I tried that were not helpful were:

6. As I look at what has helped and what has not helped, I realize that my child responds more favorably to interventions I attempt when:

7. I would talk with other parents about my child's inappropriate behavior if: *(You may choose more than one answer.)*
   - ❏ Everything else I tried failed and I want advice.
   - ❏ They seem to have their own children under control.
   - ❏ My child had done something that injured their child.
   - ❏ Their child had done something that injured my child.
   - ❏ I never would talk to other parents about my child's inappropriate behavior.

8. By talking to other parents, I would hope to learn: *(You may choose more than one answer.)*
   - ❏ That I need to try something new.
   - ❏ My other plans weren't all that off-track; I need to be more consistent.
   - ❏ Other people have had the same problem.
   - ❏ My child will grow out of the behavior.
   - ❏ I still need to find a satisfactory resolution to the problem.
   - ❏ Other.

9. I show I am pleased with my child's behavior by:

10. My child knows I am displeased with his behavior when I:

11. I teach my child to repent and forgive in this incident when I:

12. My prayer for my child's behavior at day care would be:

13. The strength I draw upon from Luke 2:48 is:

So give Your servant a discerning heart
to govern Your people and to distinguish
between right and wrong. For who is
able to govern this great people of Yours?
(1 Kings 3:9)

Two's Company

When the Lord gave Solomon the chance to ask for anything he desired, Solomon asked for a discerning heart. He then used that gift when two women who both claimed to be the mother of one baby confronted him. How often do we need a discerning heart? It can be said that we need the wisdom of Solomon to be faithful to our calling as parents. We need discernment as we encounter the variety of situations along our parenting journey with our preschoolers.

Television shows and movies make parenting seem so easy. We know what we see on the screen is fiction, of course; and the longer we are parents, the more we know how complicated it can be. We do need discernment to guide us, especially when situations involving people who interact with our children become uncomfortable. For example, how can we be certain that the baby-sitters we hire will indeed be our representatives and conform to our expectations and values? How can we be confident that the people we invite into our home will not harm our children? These people are often no more than youngsters themselves; yet we entrust to them the sacred task of caring for our children.

Do we have the same expectations of baby-sitters that we do of professional day care providers? How old should baby-sitters be? How experienced? What happens when there is trouble? What happens when baby-sitters cannot be trusted?

These are important questions. After all, when we leave our children in the care of others, it is an act of faith. It is a sacred trust that we bestow upon the baby-sitter, a trust we hope the baby-sitter will not violate. As we leave our homes, we want to be sure that our baby-sitters know they are God's representatives as well as ours. As we walk out the door and leave our children in the care of persons who are guests in our home, we pray that the Lord will keep our children in the shelter of His arms and in His protective love and care. At the same time, as we leave our children in God's hands, He calls on us to do what we have to do to ensure that our children are safe and that their welfare and best interests are taken to heart by the people we employ.

Is Sarah here?

Molly and Ron were excited. They were the new parents of their first child, a healthy baby boy named Connor. Now, two months after Connor's birth, they were feeling comfortable enough to go out on an actual date. Molly and Ron were unfamiliar with the baby-sitting scene, so Molly asked a friend, Tina, a mother who had experience with baby-sitters, to recommend a baby-sitter for their infant son.

Tina replied without hesitation, "You know, Molly, I think Sarah would be perfect for you. She's a high school junior. We've had her watch our children many times, and our kids just love her. If you wish, I'll call her first and then you can call her."

Molly was getting ready when Ron said, "Molly, I'm running late. I told Sarah we'd pick her up at 7:15 and it's already 7:30. I'll see you when I get back!" As Ron was about to put on his coat and leave, the doorbell rang. When he opened the door, Ron saw a young man who looked a little bit uncomfortable.

The young man stammered and said, "Is Sarah here?" when he saw the blank look on Ron's face, he continued, "I, uh, was told that she was going to be here."

Ron said, "No, she's not! Apparently someone told you the wrong information!" As Ron drove to Sarah's house, he wondered what he was going to say. He hadn't had time to talk with Molly, and he knew that when she found out about their visitor, she would be furious.

He pulled into Sarah's driveway and waited. When Sarah came out, she said, "Hi, I'm Sarah! Tina has told me so much about you and your wife and baby!"

All Ron said was, "I hope it was all good!" Then they drove the rest of the way to Ron and Molly's house in complete silence.

What would you do?

• What other information does Ron need before he responds to this situation?

• If you were Ron and you opened your door to be greeted by the young man in waiting, what would you have said to him that Ron did not say?

• Let's say that Ron has already left when Sarah's friend rings the doorbell and is greeted by Molly. If you were Molly, what might you have said to Sarah's friend?

• It is late; Ron and Molly have already planned their date. What are the options and the possibilities present here? Which option would you choose, and why?

• All Molly knew about Sarah is what Tina told her. What other questions might Molly have asked Tina before she agreed to ask Sarah to baby-sit?

• If you were Ron, what would you have said to Sarah after she got into the car?

• If you were Ron and you brought Sarah into your home, what would you say to Molly? When would you say it? Would you discuss the situation before you leave home or during the time you are away when both of you can sort through the options?

• What could Ron and Molly have done before their date to be prepared to deal with unexpected situations, such as the one they confronted with Sarah?

Life is filled with surprises. The phrase is well worn, but it is altogether true when it comes to leaving our children in the care of others. As we face the surprises that ultimately do come—whether they come with day care, a baby-sitter, or any other situation—it is important that we try to anticipate what our responses might be. The better we are able to anticipate such situations and how to respond to them, the less anxious we will be when surprises occur. And when the unexpected does happen, we will thoughtfully act rather than react in the heat of emotion.

No matter the surprise, it is best to act in such a way that our response helps our children and the people in whose care we entrust them. We need to act in a way that reflects our concern for fairness. At the same time, we need to communicate clearly the expectations we have for those who care for our children, as well as the expectations we have for our children when they are in the care of someone else.

It is true that we can never be completely prepared for all the unexpected situations that occur in families. We can, however, lay a strong foundation that will help us meet those uncertainties in a more proactive manner. We can share those important foundations effectively and faithfully by doing the following:

- We can know who we are as parents as well as what we want for our children.

- We can discuss the boundaries and limits we wish to impose not only on our children, but also upon those who care for our children.

- We can communicate clearly to our baby-sitters the extent of those boundaries and limits, even by placing a list of baby-sitting rules on the fridge.

- We can communicate to our baby-sitters what will happen if the boundaries we set are not respected.

- We can take appropriate action when our expectations for those who care for our children have been dishonored.

- We can ask God for wisdom to discern and identify what is helpful for our children and what is potentially harmful to them.

- We can pray for our children and for our baby-sitters as they are given responsibility for our children.

The Lord promises to be with us at all times. God encourages us to pray that He would grant us wisdom to make caring decisions that meet the challenges and the surprises that occur as a matter of course along the parenting journey. With His help, God will allow us to see that those challenges and opportunities lead to even greater manifestations of His grace.

Closing Prayer

O heavenly Father, as You granted Your servant Solomon wisdom and an understanding mind to discern between right and wrong, grant me that same wisdom and understanding as I strive to be the parent that You have called me to be. In Jesus' name. Amen.

Parent Pairs

How can parents handle the surprises that baby-sitters sometimes bring? What are the rules and expectations for those in whom they place their children's care? How can God help them be more wise and discerning when it comes to choosing baby-sitters?

Read 1 Kings 3:9 and consider the following as you discuss the **Parent Pairs** section with your spouse or with another parent.

Two's Company

(To be done with your spouse or another parent.)

1. Describe the characteristics of a baby-sitter with whom you would trust your child.

2. List at least five expectations you have for your baby-sitter:

3. How will you communicate your expectations to your baby-sitter?

4. List three possible responses to make should the baby-sitter fail to meet those expectations:

5. Think about your past baby-sitters. What are three things your children enjoyed about the baby-sitter? What are three things you valued?

6. Think about situations in which baby-sitters have not met your expectations. What could you have done differently that might have helped you avoid the situation or change your reaction to it?

7. What process do you use to check a new baby-sitter's references? Are you comfortable with your process? What would you change about it?

8. If you were to refer a baby-sitter to a friend, how would you do that? What are the most important things you would share about the baby-sitter?

   ❑ The baby-sitter's values and morals are similar to ours.

   ❑ The baby-sitter loves children.

   ❑ The baby-sitter does more than just sit with my children, she does extra housework even when I have not asked her to.

   ❑ The baby-sitter is not afraid to enforce the limits that I want enforced.

   ❑ The baby-sitter does what my children want her to do.

   ❑ The baby-sitter acts like she wants to be there.

   ❑ The baby-sitter comes with experience and references.

   ❑ My baby-sitter isn't as concerned about the money she receives as she is about the care she provides.

   ❑ Other.

9. As you think about potential baby-sitters, what sort of training do you believe they should have been given? *(Examples: CPR or a certified Red Cross baby-sitting class)*

10. I believe a fair wage for my baby-sitter would be:

11. I want my baby-sitter to say my child's nightly prayers with him or her.

   Agree   Disagree

12. My list of potential baby-sitters includes:

13. My prayer for my baby-sitter is:

14. The strength I draw upon from 1 Kings 3:9 is:

"Do not be anxious about anything, but in everything, by prayer and petition, with thanksgiving, present your requests to God. And the peace of God, which transcends all understanding, will guard your hearts and minds in Christ Jesus." (Philippians 4:6–7)

Stay in Touch

It's one thing to think about the kind of baby-sitter we want for our children and to develop a process through which we decide who the best person for that job could be. It's quite another thing, once the baby-sitter comes into our home, to guarantee that when she arrives, she will do everything we expect to provide for our child's welfare. All our parental theory and preparation to make that transition smooth for our children can be defeated in an instant.

No wonder, then, that most parents worry. For many of us, worrying is as innate as breathing. But it helps us understand our own limitations and sin. It teaches us to learn the difference between sinful worry and wise concern. Once we leave our children in the care of a baby-sitter, we want to be sure the sitter we have hired is trustworthy. We want to be free of worry and anxiety. Many parents, however, come home only to find that what they expected would happen failed to happen. Dishes were not cleaned and put away. Food was left out. Toys were not picked up. The children were still wide-awake. In short, the baby-sitting experience was not a pleasant one for the parents, the children, or even the baby-sitter.

After we have selected a baby-sitter for our children, how can we be confident that once we leave them in her care, they will be in good hands and everything will be fine? How can we communicate with our sitters how important it is to us that they do what we want them to do, as well as practice courtesy and respect for our home?

Someone once said, "The moment you become a parent is the moment you realize that your worries about your child will never end." As we deal with our worries as parents, we can place our trust in God. But struggle erupts between sinful worry and common sense! Often it is too hard to know the difference. As we trust our Lord, we can know that even in the midst of things we cannot control, our heavenly Father will be with our child and will always keep our child in His loving and protective care. Each time we leave our home, we can pray this appropriate prayer, "O God, forgive me for my worry and strengthen my trust in You. Keep my child as the apple of Your eye, under the shadow of Your almighty wing."

It's Still Busy!

Deon and Janelle were the parents of three children, all under five years of age. Theo was almost five. Karisa was three-and-a-half. Timmy was two. Deon and Janelle were looking forward to a night out and had already made arrangements with Serena, who had been their regular baby-sitter for almost a year. Serena, a high school junior, was well liked by the parents and their children.

Before Janelle left to pick up Serena, Karisa called out to her and said, "Mommy, I have a tummy ache!" Janelle gave Karisa a sip of soda, and then told her to lie on the couch. She took her temperature and it was normal.

As Janelle was driving to Serena's she said to herself, "I really don't have to worry. It's probably nothing. I have all the confidence in the world in Serena. Besides, I can call her from the restaurant, and before we go to the movie I can call her again!"

After Janelle and Deon enjoyed a great dinner, Janelle called home. The line was busy. She thought nothing of it. Then, after they bought their tickets for the movie, she called Serena again and again heard a busy signal. She said to Deon, "That really bothers me! The line is still busy. I hope everything is all right! You don't think she's on-line using our computer to chat with her friends, do you?"

"Don't worry!" Deon said. "Serena wouldn't do that. Besides, she loves our kids and knows we would be really upset if we wanted to call and couldn't get through."

"But I need to talk to her!" Janelle exclaimed.

When Deon and Janelle returned home, it was 11:30 P.M. Serena was on the computer. Janelle discovered that Karisa was still awake, and by this time her tummy ache had moved to her lower right abdominal region. She felt Karisa's forehead, and it was very warm. Upon that discovery, Janelle glared at Serena and said ...

What would you do?

- Finish the conversation, assuming that you are Janelle and you are about to speak to Serena.

- What might Janelle and Deon have done before they went out that would have been helpful for everyone?

- Identify the problems or issues here. Share with your spouse or the group how you would address each issue. Decide who is the appropriate person to address each issue.

- What do you think Janelle needs from Deon when she says, "That really bothers me. The line is still busy. I hope everything is all right!"?

- Deon seems to ignore Janelle's anxiety. How might Deon have been more helpful in this situation?

- Deon and Janelle appear unwilling to make a decision about the situation. What might they have done differently to arrive at a decision sooner? At what point do you think Deon should have listened to Janelle's anxiety and acted on it. What were their options for action?

- When Deon and Janelle arrive home, they find that Karisa's symptoms have worsened. What do these symptoms seem to signify?

- How can we minimize the worry and anxiety we experience as we leave our children in the care of a baby-sitter? How should we react when we discover that the baby-sitter has not met our expectations or done what we had hoped he or she would do?

- How does this become an opportunity to teach the baby-sitter the consequences of her actions?

- How does this become an opportunity to teach the baby-sitter about sin and forgiveness?

Answers to these questions may not be easy, but as we ask them, we can trust that by relying on God's strength and exercising our common sense, we can lessen our anxiety. We can start by:

- Letting baby-sitters know that we will periodically check in with them throughout the evening, so it is important that the phone be free.

- Making a list of the things we want our baby-sitter to accomplish while we are gone. We can also tell her that we will ask how things went when we arrive back home.

- Being more direct about what is off limits. For example, we may not want our baby-sitter to go on-line or use the phone at all when we are not home. We may point out what food is for the baby-sitter and what food is off-limits. And we may set limits on the baby-sitter having friends over.

- Leaving detailed instructions about how we can be reached and when we would expect our sitters to try to contact us.

- Leaving alternate numbers with our sitters in case there is an emergency and we cannot be reached and being specific about our expectations in an emergency.

- Explaining to her that she is there in your place and you are there on behalf of God. Help her to understand her called vocation as a baby-sitter.

When we take the time to be thorough and well prepared, not only will our anxiety lessen, but our baby-sitter's anxiety will lessen as well. Even when events happen that cause us uneasy moments, we can remember that God forgives us and strengthens us to trust Him. God cares for our children and for us with an everlasting love.

Closing Prayer

Loving God, I know that You have invited me to cast all my worries and cares upon You because Your love for me never ends. Forgive me for my lack of trust. Grant me wisdom to parent the child You have given me, to remember to give You all my worries and cares. Help me know that You will take my worries and cares and will replace them with the confidence that You remain with my child always. In Jesus' name. Amen.

Parent Pairs

What are your expectations of those who come to your home to care for your child? What can you do to lessen your anxiety as you leave your child in the care of a baby-sitter? Read Philippians 4:6–7 and consider the following questions as you discuss the **Parent Pairs** section with your spouse or with another parent.

Stay in Touch

(To be done with your spouse or another parent.)

1. My expectations for a baby-sitter are: *(Rank in order of importance with #1 being the most important, then #2, #3, etc.)*

    ___ My baby-sitter needs to do additional housework while in my home.

    ___ My baby-sitter needs only to clean up the messes that happen while he or she is in my home.

    ___ I don't care about housework; I want my baby-sitter to spend quality time with my children and cater to their needs.

    ___ I want my baby-sitter to be mature enough to be able to take care of the unexpected.

    ___ I want my baby-sitter to know C.P.R.

    ___ I expect my baby-sitter not to use the computer or talk on the phone while she or he is baby-sitting.

    ___ I expect my baby-sitter to say prayers with my children at bedtime.

2. When I have a baby-sitter, I promise that I will: *(Rank in order of importance with #1 being the most important, then #2, #3, etc.)*

    ___ Always let the baby-sitter know where I am and how I can be reached.

    ___ Have a list of telephone numbers of responsible adults to call in case the baby-sitter is unable to reach me.

    ___ Make sure the baby-sitter is aware of any medical needs my children may have.

    ___ Be clear about what time I am coming home and what to do if I am not home at the hour I promise to be.

    ___ Be clear about expectations I have for my own children as well as for the baby-sitter.

    ___ Promise to call the baby-sitter if I have a change of plans.

3. The times when the baby-sitting experience has gone the most smoothly have been:

4. The times when the experience has not gone well have been:

5. The differences in those two experiences taught me:

6. In case of a medical emergency, I would give my baby-sitter these instructions:

7. In the event that my baby-sitter cannot reach me, I want her to notify these people:

8. I have a list of specific instructions that deal with emergencies as well as alternate people to contact who are readily available for my baby-sitter to see. I also make sure that the baby-sitter has read those instructions before I leave.

   Agree   **Disagree**

9. If I could tell another parent how to have a successful baby-sitting experience, I would share at least these two pieces of advice:

10. The strength I gain from Philipians 4:6–7 is:

Love is patient, love is kind. It does not
envy, it does not boast, it is not proud.
It is not rude, it is not self-seeking, it is
not easily angered, it keeps no record of
wrongs. ... It always protects, always trusts,
always hopes, always perseveres.
(1 Corinthians 13:4–5, 7)

But She Likes You!

Love makes the world go 'round, or so they say. As Christians, we love one another because Jesus first loved us. We try to instill that attitude in our children, so we work hard to teach them to demonstrate that love and share it with others. When they don't, we become frustrated. Sometimes, we let ourselves believe that our children are a reflection of us, our values, and our beliefs. When our children fail to show love to one another—or even show dislike toward others—we are tempted to blame ourselves for our inability to communicate such an important concept.

As we read 1 Corinthians, especially the thirteenth chapter, we learn about a type of love called *agape*. Agape, in Greek, means unconditional love. Keep in mind that agape love is something God does perfectly and we cannot do. It is best understood in God's suffering on the cross. Only He could pay for sin. Forgiveness is the context of agape. Remembering this can help us in many situations we face as parents, such as when our children do not show Christian love to others.

Consider the qualities parents look for in the perfect baby-sitter. She is dependable. She likes children. She has good references. So the parents go out for an evening confidently. However, upon their return, they discover that not everything went as well as they had hoped. The parents learn that the sitter they thought was perfect was not a good choice after all. Many parents who have ignored this critique have found their children's feelings of dislike grow more intense if they hire the same sitter for another time.

Consider how Jesus' command to love one another might guide us when our children react negatively to sitters. Each time we introduce our children to new people, we can help them learn to show that kind of love. We can teach them that all people—even those we don't choose as our friends—are loved unconditionally by God through the redeeming work of His Son.

But what's wrong with her?

Tara and Travis Jones were the parents of two boys: Sam, who was five, and Tyler, who was three. The first time Tara and Travis hired Jenny, they came home to a seemingly normal situation. The boys were in bed and the house was neat. Jenny was in a very good mood when Travis drove her home. As they were driving to Jenny's house, Travis asked Jenny how things had gone with the boys. Jenny replied that there were no problems at all and that things had gone very well.

The next morning when Sam and Tyler were eating breakfast, Tara asked Sam, "How did you like Jenny?"

"She was a dumb baby-sitter!" Sam answered.

"A dumb baby-sitter?" Tara asked. "What made her a dumb baby-sitter?"

"I don't know!" Sam answered. "She was just dumb. I didn't like her at all!"

"But I know she likes you!" Tara said.

"Well, I don't like her! I hope I never see her again!" was Sam's reply.

"Well, Sam, you better get used to it! Your dad and I are going out next Friday and Jenny is going to be your baby-sitter again!"

"I don't want her!" said Sam.

Tara looked at Tyler and said, "Tyler, how did you like Jenny last night?" At that, Tyler began to cry.

Tara threw up her arms and called out, "Travis, I think you and I need to talk! And we need to talk right now!"

What would you do?

- What information might Tara need to try to resolve this situation?

- Tara's first question to Sam was, "How did you like Jenny?" How important do you think it is that children like their baby-sitters?

- Is the question about liking Jenny the most helpful question to ask Sam? What might be a better question to ask Sam about Jenny?

- Sam called Jenny a "dumb baby-sitter." What are some of the reasons a five-year-old might call a baby-sitter dumb? If you were Sam's parent, which reasons would give you cause to reconsider whether Jenny should be hired to baby-sit again?

- After questioning Sam, Tara turned to Tyler and asked him the same question. What other questions might Tara ask Tyler to find out how the experience went? How would these questions be different than the ones she asked Sam?

- After talking to both boys, Tara seemed to be extremely frustrated. Is Tara creating an unnecessary crisis? What could Tara do to help her more effectively sort through her feelings and more objectively analyze the opinions the boys have given?

- Imagine you are Travis and you sense Tara's frustration with the boys' dislike for Jenny. How would you respond to Tara? What would you say?

It is unreasonable to expect that our children will like every person they meet. Nor is it possible to convince them to like everyone. When our children do not like someone, a sitter for example, it is important for us to try, patiently, to understand the reason behind their reaction. It could be as simple as the fact that this baby-sitter strictly enforced the limits we set. It could be that our children's previous baby-sitter was no longer available and our children are expressing disappointment over the loss. It could be that our children are right: The chemistry between them and the baby-sitter is not good.

How can we sort through all the information we need to decide whether to hire the baby-sitter again? What is the most helpful strategy for alleviating our stress and helping our children to have a positive experience with a baby-sitter?

To address these issues, it is helpful to ask our children direct questions about their experience, such as:

> • What games did the baby-sitter play with you?
>
> • What television programs did you watch?
>
> • Did you have a bedtime snack?
>
> • Was anyone else in the house?
>
> • Did the sitter spend time on the computer or the phone?

Our children's answers to questions such as these will enable us to make better decisions as to whether we will rehire that particular baby-sitter.

We bring this discussion to a close the same way we began. It is helpful to remember that what we cannot do, God does perfectly for us. Therefore, when we do not show Christ's love as we ought and when our children do not like others when we want them to, we can be thankful that God still loves us.

It is important to engage our children in experiencing God's love. One place to experience His grace is in the community of believers, the body of Christ. Through worship, Sunday school, and a variety of activities, our children will meet many people and will learn about their heavenly Father's unconditional love and grace. That grace covers us whenever we feel inadequate, confused, or do not know how to respond. For God's love for us always protects, always trusts, always hopes, always perseveres.

Closing Prayer

Loving Lord God, teach me to love my child in the same way that You love me—completely and totally. As I deal with their concerns about baby-sitters and other people, help me to affirm my children and love them for who they are, baptized children that are given to me from Your gracious hand. I pray in Your Son's holy name. Amen.

Parent Pairs

How much input should preschoolers have in selecting a baby-sitter? How much and what kind of information can our children give that is necessary to best determine the effectiveness of the baby-sitter we have hired? How can God's love, comfort, and forgiveness strengthen us as we make important decisions about our children's care?

Read 1 Corinthians 13:4–5, 7 and consider the following questions as you discuss the **Parent Pairs** section with your spouse or with another parent.

But She Likes You!

(To be done with your spouse or another parent.)

1. I believe my preschoolers: *(Choose one.)*

   ❑ Should have significant input in choosing their baby-sitter.

   ❑ Should have no say in who is hired as their baby-sitter.

   ❑ Should be listened to but still have no say in who is hired as their baby-sitter.

   ❑ Should accept whatever is decided about who their baby-sitter is.

   ❑ Other.

2. If my child did not like the baby-sitter: *(Choose one.)*

   ❑ I would never hire the baby-sitter again.

   ❑ I would call the sitter and find out more information about what happened.

   ❑ I would ask my children direct questions to get more details about what had happened.

   ❑ I would ignore them because I would see their comments as a manipulative attempt to make me stay home.

   ❑ Other.

3. Rank in order of importance the questions you would ask a baby-sitter at the end of the evening. *(Rank in order of importance with #1 being the most important, then #2, #3, etc.)*

   ____Are there any messages?

   ____How did it go at bedtime?

   ____What games did you play with the children?

   ____What did the children eat?

   ____Did you have any visitors?

   ____How long did it take for the children to settle down before bedtime?

   ____Did anything unusual happen that I should know about?

   ____What television programs did the children watch?

4. Rank in order of importance the questions you would ask your children after a baby-sitter had stayed with them:

   ____Did you have fun?

   ____What games did you play?

   ____What treats did you eat?

   ____What TV programs did you watch?

   ____When did you go to bed?

   ____I don't usually ask questions. I don't believe in interrogating my children about their baby-sitters.

   ____Other.

5. I usually give baby-sitters detailed instructions about what they are to do with my children and when they are to complete those tasks.

     Agree   Disagree

6. I tell my baby-sitters that I expect them to complete the tasks that I provide for them.

     Agree   Disagree

7. I tell my baby-sitters that I will check with my children about how their night went.

     Agree   Disagree

8. I would invite a baby-sitter to return if:

9. I would not invite a baby-sitter to return if:

10. Share an instance when you did not rehire a baby-sitter and why.

11. I help my children understand how they are to show love and forgiveness to others because Christ first loved them by:

12. The strength I draw upon from 1 Corinthians 13:4–5, 7 is:

He will not let your foot slip—He who watches over you will not slumber; indeed, He who watches over Israel will neither slumber nor sleep. (Psalm 121:3–4)

Midnight Blues

As parents we take all the burdens and responsibilities of parenting upon our own shoulders. We believe that being successful is entirely based upon what we do. Considering the stress of this expectation, it is a gift of grace to remember that God, our perfect Father in heaven, never slumbers nor does He sleep. He called you to be a child of Israel in your Baptism. And, therefore, our loving heavenly Father always forgives and has sealed you in His promises.

Being aware of our heavenly Father's promises is reassuring when the baby arrives and parents begin to experience the various lifestyle changes this arrival brings. Perhaps one of the greatest changes to which new parents must adjust is the change in sleeping patterns a child can cause. Indeed, it is a landmark day when a mom or dad announces to friends or family, "Adrienne slept through the entire night. She went to bed at 8:00 P.M. and didn't get up until 6:00 A.M. It was absolutely wonderful."

Often, just when parents think their lives have returned to normal and they believe they really will enjoy an entire night's sleep, something happens to disrupt their child's sleeping patterns, bringing everyone back to square one. For some unknown reason, their little one awakens regularly during the night and has a difficult time falling asleep again. What is a parent to do?

Answers to that question can be as difficult to find. Each child has a different rhythm. Each child responds to his own needs, as well as to his parents, in a different way. Parenting styles differ. A firstborn may do a better job of "training" his parents to get up in the middle of the night. However, by the time child number two comes along, parents are not so readily trained. The subtle clash of wills becomes a little more intense. Parental anxiety has eased somewhat and Mom and Dad are more willing to let their second child cry a bit longer.

Even when parents believe they will never enjoy a good night's sleep again, it is important to remember from where we draw our strength. The answer for the psalmist was that strength came not from the hills; strength comes from the Lord who never sleeps. May our Lord continue to provide needed rest and baptismal refreshment for us as children and parents alike.

I wish I knew!

Juan and Carla had tried to have children for five years. Just when they thought there was no longer hope, Maria was born. Juan and Carla were elated. They were overjoyed when they brought Maria home to the new nursery they had decorated with so much love and care. For the first few weeks Maria would awaken every three or four hours. After changing and feeding her, she would go back to sleep, but the whole process would take at least an hour. As a result, whoever got up with her would be exhausted the next day. Eventually, to her parent's relief, Maria began sleeping through the night without waking.

A few months later, Juan and Carla were in the middle of a deep sleep when they were startled awake by a shrieking scream coming from Maria's room. They jumped up from bed and found that Maria had pulled herself up and was standing inside her crib. Tears were streaming down her face as she stood shaking the railing. Juan and Carla were alarmed; they had no idea why Maria was crying but it was obvious that their little girl was uncomfortable. The next day, Carla took Maria to the doctor and discovered that she had an ear infection in both ears. Carla was assured that with medicine, Maria's illness would be cured soon and life could return to normal for the family.

The normalcy, however, did not return. Four weeks later, a tired and haggard-looking Carla ran into her friend Danielle at the grocery store and said, "Danielle, I can't take any more of this. I absolutely don't know what I am going to do! I mean, we waited so long for Maria to be born. Now, I'm not sure if I'll ever get any sleep again, and I am so exhausted every day. Nobody told me it would be like this. Maria keeps waking up in the middle of the night and she has such a difficult time settling down after that. What in the world am I going to do? I get so frustrated and angry with her. And I feel so guilty when I do."

Danielle looked at Carla and said, "Let her cry, Carla; you've got to let her cry!"

What would you do?

• If you were Carla, what options would you consider before just letting Maria cry?

• Although Maria has been ill recently, what might be other reasons for her waking up in the middle of the night?

• Carla stated, "I get so frustrated and angry with her (Maria). And I feel so guilty when I do." How might you have responded to Carla's feelings of frustration, anger, and guilt? What importance does Baptism and forgiveness play for Carla? What do the Lord's promises to the children of Israel have to do with Carla?

• Nothing is said about Juan. What kind of support do you think Juan might offer Carla as they dealt with Maria's midnight blues? What support might Juan need from Carla?

• Danielle tells Carla to let Maria cry. Do you think this is an effective response? Why or why not?

- If you were Carla and decided to take Danielle's advice, how long would you let Maria cry each night? For how many nights would you let her cry before you attempted a different strategy?

- At what age do you think that it is all right to let an infant or toddler cry his or her way to sleep?

Adequate sleep is a very important part of a healthy life. We need sleep. The disciples needed sleep the night Jesus asked them to watch and pray with Him in the garden of Gethsemane. Even our Lord needed sleep when His ministry on earth was physically and mentally demanding. When we get enough sleep, we have the energy and enthusiasm to meet the challenges of the day ahead. With the ability to meet those challenges, we learn and grow from our experiences and we nurture others in their daily lives as well.

When we are deprived of sleep, even if it is because of our precious children, the challenges of parenting can become burdens, not opportunities. Joys are displaced by obligations. Fatigue becomes frustration. When we do not get enough sleep because our child is keeping us awake, we need to consider all the possible causes and solutions. Some may include:

- Remembering to follow up with our child's pediatrician to make sure we are not missing any health factors that may be causing our child's sleeplessness.

- Examining our own sources of stress and how we might be conveying them to our child. If we are stressed and anxious when our children get up in the middle of the night, they will sense that anxiety. The more anxious we are, the less likely our child is to return to sleep very quickly.

- Tracking our children's diet to make sure they are eating enough throughout the day. Our child's diet can affect his sleeping pattern.

- Looking for signs of new teeth that might be causing discomfort.

- Changing some patterns, such as midnight feedings and the amount of time we allow our child to remain awake in the middle of the night. (This is difficult to do. Our initial response to fussing is to comfort them. However, by comforting them too often, we may be allowing them to develop patterns that are very difficult to change.)

- Continuing to ask God to strengthen us as we travel our parenting journey with this particular little one. As we pray with our child at bedtime, include in that prayer a petition to God that our child sleeps soundly through the night.

It is not only our frame of mind or attitude that is affected by the amount of sleep we get, lack of sleep also affects the way we respond to our children, our spouse, and others. That is why it is important to do what we can to ensure that we will be as well rested as possible so we can be in the best disposition to act lovingly and responsibly. (That may mean even calling a friend or relative to baby-sit while we take a needed nap.) Rest, then, can be one way to lead a rewarding life as the parent of a little one who needs our love and our care.

When none of that is possible, and sometimes it seems impossible, remember that you are a chosen member of God's family in your Baptism. As you become frustrated, angry, and guilty, know that the Father who never sleeps always forgives. God remains our Father. We are free to call upon Him as our source of strength and help at any time, in every place, with every situation.

Closing Prayer

Loving God, I know that You neither slumber nor sleep. As I deal with my own lack of sleep that parenthood can bring, give me patience, courage, strength, and understanding to know that because of You, heavenly Father, I can be still and trust that Your love for me and for my children is constant. Thank You for choosing me in my Baptism, a soothing source of forgiveness. In Jesus' name, I pray. Amen.

Parent Pairs

What happens when you begin to feel as though you will never sleep again? How do you establish a regular sleep pattern for your child that not only gives her the rest she needs but allows you to get the rest you need as well? How can you determine what your child needs to help develop her own healthy sleep pattern?

Read Psalm 121:4–5 and consider the following questions as you discuss the **Parent Pairs** section with your spouse or another parent.

Midnight Blues

(To be done with your spouse or another parent.)

1. In order to feel like a well-rested human being, I need at least ⎯⎯ hours of sleep each night.

2. When I fail to receive the sleep I need, I become: *(Check the ones that apply to you.)*
   - ☐ Extremely crabby at anyone who gets in my way.
   - ☐ Depressed and wonder about my purpose or role in life.
   - ☐ More worried or anxious about everyday events than I normally would be.
   - ☐ Depressed, feeling like the worst parent in the world.
   - ☐ So tired that I hardly have energy to think about anything or anyone else.
   - ☐ Silly. In fact, the more tired I am, the sillier I tend to become.
   - ☐ So critical of myself that I know my feelings, self-esteem, and self-worth get depleted.
   - ☐ None of this applies to me because I am never affected by a lack of sleep.
   - ☐ Other.

3. Describe how the lack of sleep may hinder your parenting abilities.

4. Describe two times you tried to keep going despite a lack of sleep. How was your child affected by your lack of sleep? How were your relationships affected, especially with your spouse? How was your productivity at your job or profession affected?

5. Describe three ways you have dealt with your child's sleep disturbances in the past.

6. What was helpful about these strategies?

7. What was not so helpful?

8. What, if anything, do you need to do to change your own nightly sleep pattern? What can you do to get more rest?

9. If you were to advise new parents about dealing with their children's lack of sleep, what would you say?

10. The best advice anyone gave about your child's sleeplessness at night was:

11. Name three people you can depend upon who would be willing to help you get more sleep.

12. In a revised plan for dealing with your child's sleep disturbances, three things you might do differently are:

13. My prayer for my child to sleep soundly through the night is:

14. The strength I draw upon from Psalm 121:4–5 is:

When Jesus saw this, He was indignant. He said to them, "Let the little children come to Me, and do not hinder them, for the kingdom of God belongs to such as these." (Mark 10:14)

Who's Been Sleeping in My Bed?

We know that Jesus welcomed children and held them up as examples of membership in the kingdom of God. In our role as parents, however, we know there are times and places when young children are not all that welcome. And sleeping in our bed may be one of them. At such times, we strive to be consistent in our attempts to help our children know their limits and be secure within their own boundaries. This is the difference between the family of God and the family at home. One is about daily forgiveness and heaven, the other is about daily order and boundaries. This is a great time to teach our child about the difference between being an adult or child, a mom or dad, and a husband or wife.

As an infant grows, the day comes when he takes a big step away from the confines of the crib—sleeping in a big bed. As the toddler transitions from crib to bed, he finds a new sense of freedom and adventure. Now he has the freedom to explore and to discover new things in the dark; the power to get out of bed on his own and get a drink of water, go to the bathroom, or listen to conversations from the hallway or the top of the stairs. This opportunity to stretch limits imposed by parents is a test of how far Mom or Dad are willing to be pushed before consequences are given.

With this newfound freedom, the toddler finds different ways of dealing with stressors. While in the crib, when his sleep was disturbed, the child would cry, shake the sides of the crib, or occasionally take a startled tumble or two onto the floor. But now that he is freed from the barrier of the crib, when his sleep is disturbed, the toddler may walk into Mom and Dad's room and seek comfort. Then, a groggy parent either leads the toddler back to his bed or gathers him into the parent's own bed.

It is easy for parents to see this phase as just that—a period in the child's life when he or she is testing the boundaries. However, an issue that needs to be addressed is the definition of family. The parents and the child have become a family. The family struggles to determine when the child is included in that constellation and when he needs to be separate, away from the parents, to explore his own identity. Making that determination can be very difficult indeed.

There are no easy answers. As the parents and child seek to find balance and boundaries, they can rely on the strength and comfort in the miracle that through Baptism they are members of God's family. They are reinforced by the blessings of that family through the gifts that God gives at church. No matter how intense the struggles are within their own family, the gifts that God gives of His Word and the sacramental life are a steadying and comforting influence.

Will you please roll over?

Sue and Tom were the parents of two school-age boys, Allen and John, when Missy was born. Like many parents, they discovered that their ways of parenting Allen and John had relaxed a bit by the time Missy was a toddler. After all, Sue and Tom were more experienced parents and not as anxious and nervous about the entire process as they were with the older children.

When she was a year old, Missy graduated to a big bed and was proud to be like her big brothers. A few months later, in the midst of a deep sleep, Tom nudged Sue and said, "Sue will you please roll over? If you come any closer, I'm going to fall off the bed."

"I can't" Sue said.

"Why?" Tom replied.

"Because Missy is in bed with us and I can't move her!" Sue said, feeling her frustration begin to rise.

"Take her back to bed! We didn't let the boys sleep with us! Why are we letting Missy do it? You know, they say that if we let her do this once, we'll have an even greater problem breaking her of this habit!" Tom implored.

"If you're so concerned about what 'they' say," Sue answered, "you can take her to back to bed yourself!"

Tom groaned, got out of bed, picked Missy up, and carried her back to her room.

When he returned, he said, "There; tomorrow night it's your turn!"

What would you do?

> • By their own admission, Sue and Tom were more relaxed in their parenting of Missy. What causes parents to become more relaxed after their second or third child is born?
>
> • How might that sense of being relaxed be helpful, especially for Missy? How might it be not as helpful for Missy or for Allen and John?
>
> • We are given no information about the limits Sue and Tom set for Missy when she made her transition to a big bed. How can parents communicate limits to a child as young as Missy?
>
> • In some cultures, the practice of the family bed, where everyone sleeps together, is common. What might make that practice acceptable? Why might other cultures consider the family bed not helpful or acceptable?
>
> • Obviously, the middle of the night when both parents are tired and sleep is disturbed is not a good time to talk about this issue. Let's assume Tom

and Sue agree to discuss it before Missy's bedtime the next evening. What options might help them resolve the situation? How might Tom and Sue support each other in the decisions they make?

• What do you think is happening with Missy that causes her to want to sleep in her parents' bed? What do you think Missy needs from her parents?

• What other ways can Tom and Sue address Missy's needs short of letting her sleep in their bed?

Little ones with sad faces gazing longingly into their mom or dad's sleepy eyes are hard to resist. It becomes even more difficult for parents to refuse their children when they are asleep in a warm bed and face a struggle when they take their toddler back to their own bed. Understandably then, it can be easy for parents to take the path of least resistance and let their child sleep with them.

Whether our resistance is as strong or not as strong as we would like, asking these questions might be helpful:

• When do we include our child in our activities and which activities should be off limits?

• How can this be an opportunity to teach our child the difference between mom/dad and husband/wife boundaries?

• How do we communicate these limits to our child?

• What is the pattern of behavior I want to teach my child that benefits my child the most?

• What is the pattern of behavior I want my child to learn that is most beneficial to us as parents?

• What are other ways I can communicate to my child that he or she is valued, precious, and loved?

• What family rituals have I established around bedtime that assure my child he or she is a secure part of our family even during sleep hours?

Answering these questions helps us realize that what our children want from us is affirmation of safety, that the boundaries around them and us are secure. We trust that our ability to set firm boundaries will not only help them as they develop a sense of security and strength, but also that our children will be blessed by those very boundaries that we set. They will grow up to learn how to be a parent and a spouse.

As we deal with such issues in the development of our immediate family, we can be thankful for the larger family into which we have been baptized. We are thankful that we can experience that family through the gifts we receive at church weekly. It is from our family in Christ that we receive love, care, and nurture. In the meal of Holy Communion we receive forgiveness and the victorious resurrected body and blood of Jesus. There, in that Holy Meal, He gives us what He secured on the cross and thereby He securely binds us together with God, our heavenly Father, and with our children and our brothers and sisters in Christ as well. May that family in Christ encourage us and give us joy as we continue to build our family through the gift of our children.

Closing Prayer

O God, Your Son took the little children in His arms and blessed them. Help me to set wise boundaries for my children that I might be a blessing to them on this day and always. In Jesus' name. Amen.

Parent Pairs

What are the important boundaries you want to reinforce for your children's benefit as well as for yours? What specific boundaries do you want to impose on your child while she learns to sleep in her own bed? How might you reassure your child about the limits you set when it comes to sleeping patterns?

Read Mark 10:14 and consider the following questions as you discuss the **Parent Pairs** section with your spouse or with another parent.

Who's Been Sleeping in My Bed?

(To be done with your spouse or another parent.)

1. Name three of your family's favorite activities.

2. Name three activities from which your child is excluded because of either age or your need to spend time together as a couple.

3. What rituals do you practice that let your child know the welfare and strength of the family are secure?

4. Describe your child's bedtime ritual. How do you incorporate prayer, Scripture, and faith talk as a part of the ritual?

5. If my toddler wanted to sleep in my bed, I would: *(Choose one response that comes the closest to your feeling.)*

   ❑ Welcome my child with open arms because it gets mighty cold at night.

   ❑ Ignore my child and hope he or she would get the hint.

   ❑ Let my child sleep in my bed only once.

   ❑ Decide what do to depending on the situation. Perhaps my child is frightened or ill and needs my comfort.

   ❑ Immediately take my child back to bed.

   ❑ Other.

6. Boundaries between parents and children should be preserved, and because they are, the parental bed is off limits.

   Agree   Disagree

7. If I wanted to change my toddler's habit of sleeping in my bed, I would: *(You may choose more than one answer.)*
   - ❑ First try to figure out what my child's needs are.
   - ❑ Try to give my child more attention during the day.
   - ❑ Have my child sleep only in his or her bed.
   - ❑ Slowly ease my child from his or her habit.
   - ❑ Other.

8. List three boundaries between a parent and a toddler that you believe are important enough to be enforced.

9. List three boundaries between a parent and a toddler you believe are flexible.

10. One boundary I have set for my child with which I need to be more flexible and understanding is:

11. When I think about one boundary I have set for my child that I have failed to enforce, it is:

12. After thinking about that boundary, my revised plan for enforcing it includes:

13. What are the similarites and differences between the family of God and your immediate family?

14. The strength I gain from Mark 10:14 is:

O LORD, You have searched me and You know me. You know when I sit and when I rise; You perceive my thoughts from afar. You discern my going out and my lying down; You are familiar with all my ways. (Psalm 139:1–3)

But You Need a Nap!

"You deserve a break today!" a popular commercial for a fast food restaurant once sang out. The most familiar break known to parents and children is the nap. The nap gives growing children a chance to regroup and rest from the activities of the morning and to re-energize for the rest of day. God knows parents need breaks as well. He recognizes our fatigue and the frustration that may result from it. As God does this, He continually renews and refreshes us through His Word and the sacramental life.

Naptime allows parents to take a break from their children and either enjoy the solitude of the moment or take on tasks that are difficult to complete when children are present. Thus the nap benefits both parents and children. It becomes an important part of the structure of the day. Consequently, when the nap cycle is interrupted or when children refuse to take a nap, chaos can often result.

As we talk about naps, we remember the concept of the Sabbath from the Old Testament. The Sabbath was observed as a day of rest, a day to recognize the presence of God on earth and His work, and a day to give back to God what He had given to His people ... their daily bread. As we enforce naptime for our children, and even as they outgrow that need, it is good for us to remember the purpose of the Sabbath and teach our children, regardless of their age, the importance of dedicating time to rest, church, and service to others. Also, no matter where we are with our children in the nap process, it is never too early to begin to teach them (and to remember ourselves) that while we sleep, we remain in God's constant, protective, loving care, and baptismal grace. As He wills, He will bring us to the end of our children's nap cycle or the beginning of another day. The peace and renewal we receive from a good nap or night's sleep reminds us of the peace and renewal we receive from God by faith in Him.

It's time

Sarah was almost three years old, the youngest of four children. Sarah's mom, Joan, had been laid off from her job and decided that she would take time to be with Sarah and enjoy life as a stay-at-home mom for a while before returning to the job market. That was perfectly all right with Ethan, her husband. It made life less stressful in the mornings and he didn't have to worry about picking Sarah up from day care after work in the evenings.

Things went smoothly the first two months. But about the beginning of Joan's third month at home, she noticed a change. It happened one afternoon when she had tucked Sarah in for an afternoon nap. After she had gone downstairs, she heard little footsteps above. Quietly, she went back upstairs and peeked into Sarah's room. Sarah was playing with her dolls. If this would have been a one-time occurrence, Joan would not have made an issue of it, but it continued every day for weeks. Joan shares her story:

"My other children were good nappers. They didn't give up naps until they were almost four years old. So I guess I'm not convinced Sarah is out of the napping stage, yet.

"I was glad for some time off from work. I thought it would be the best of both worlds: I would have time with Sarah and I would have time for myself. My concern is that if I don't get time for myself, I'm not going to have good, quality time with Sarah either. I've tried postponing her nap until later in the afternoon, but then she refuses to go to bed at night. I've tried to develop a ritual for naptime, like reading her a story, singing a song with her, but that doesn't work either. The trouble with all of this is that I'm crabby, and Sarah gets crabby too.

"I am so discouraged. I told Ethan the other day that I'm thinking of looking for a job again. Maybe it's me! Maybe it's Sarah! All I know is that she doesn't want to nap. I spend more time putting her back to bed than I do on all the unfinished work that needs to be done around here.

"Tomorrow, I'm going to dust off my résumé!"

What would you do?

- As you listen to Joan's lament, identify the issues that need to be discussed.

- If Joan sees Sarah's nap as an opportunity for some quiet time for herself, what are other ways she might find that quiet time?

- What other information would be useful for us to analyze why Sarah seems to have decided to give up naps before age three?

- How could Joan's remark, "My other children were good nappers," not be a helpful comment in her attempt to deal with Sarah?

- Joan seems to use Sarah's unwillingness to take naps as a reason to go back to work. What makes that a good reason? A bad reason? If you were Joan, what reason would you use for returning to the work force?

- Joan seems to imply that nothing will get done around the house if she doesn't do it. What should Joan expect from Ethan in this situation that would help relieve her stress?

- Joan mentioned that she had changed Sarah's rituals before putting her down for a nap. How important are rituals that revolve around bedtime or naptime?

- If you were Joan's best friend, what advice would you give to her?

Time alone is important for parents. Time alone and nap times are necessary for toddlers too. The dilemma for us as parents comes when we are faced with the reality of a toddler who is ready to give up the tradition of the nap before we are willing to let them give it up. When their timing does not match our timing, power struggles occur and problems arise. In the midst of such power struggles, we need to focus on what our children need and what we need. We can do that in a much better way, if we:

- *Examine the naptime rituals we have established with our toddler.* As we do, we can ask ourselves these questions: Do I place my toddler down for his or her nap at the same time each day? Have I changed rituals, such as a different snack, failed to read a story, or played a different game?

- *Read the signs my toddler gives about his or her naptime.* Has my toddler started to take shorter naps? Has his or her resistance to the idea increased?

- *Evaluate our need to have our toddler take his or her nap.* What tasks do I need to accomplish while my toddler sleeps? Are there other times when I could accomplish the same tasks? Do I use naptime as a period when I find some needed rest as well? Are there other ways I can get that same rest?

- *Encourage a positive, fun outlook that helps my toddler look forward to taking a nap.* Am I communicating to my toddler that this is an experience they *get* to do, rather than an experience they *have* to do? Toddlers can sense the difference in our attitude by the tone of our words and by our body language. Our toddler can sense our tension or anxiety by the way we touch him and hold him and try to enforce the limits we impose.

We all need a balance between alone time and together time, between our periods of wakefulness and sleep. As we pursue that balance, may we remember the God who knows us and our thoughts. May we teach our children the value not only of rest, but the importance of the Sabbath. The New Testament Sabbath is still about God's presence on earth. His presence to forgive us in water and Word, in body and blood. That's because He knows us and our need for mercy, forgiveness, and strength. May we be mindful of the God who knew our needs and responded with Jesus. May we center ourselves and our lives on the God who continues to seek us out through His Word and the Sacraments.

As we remember the God who remembers us, the God whose Son, Jesus Christ, took time away from His work to rest and sleep, may we trust that our Lord will help us find rest as well. He will grant us and our children wisdom so we might find a happy compromise that will allow all of us to get the rest we need and to be satisfied with the rest we are given.

Closing Prayer

O God, I thank You for knowing me completely and totally. Help me, especially when I need rest, to have the patience to be an understanding parent so I might do Your will and be Your faithful servant. In Your Son's name, I pray. Amen.

Parent Pairs

How much rest does your toddler need? How much rest do you need? What are important rituals you and your toddler share before naptime? When is a toddler ready to stop taking naps? How can you be a patient parent when it is difficult for you and your child to get the rest you both need?

Read Psalm 139:1–3 and consider the following questions as you discuss the **Parent Pairs** section with your spouse or with another parent.

But You Need a Nap!

(To be done with your spouse or another parent.)

1. I believe it is important to incorporate rituals into my toddler's naptime.

    Agree   Disagree

2. Two important rituals I share with my toddler before naptime are: *(If you presently do not have a naptime ritual, use this space to think about the rituals you would like to share with your toddler.)*

3. Naptime and bedtime rituals are important because: *(You may choose more than one answer.)*
    - ☐ They bring a sense of order into the life of my toddler.
    - ☐ They remind my toddler about the unique experience of taking a nap.
    - ☐ They serve as a special way for me to bond with my toddler.
    - ☐ They create a lasting, fond memory for my toddler as he or she continues to grow.
    - ☐ They serve as a valuable teaching time for my toddler to learn about the Sabbath and where God comes to us now.
    - ☐ Other.

4. Time alone for me during the day is: *(You may choose more than one answer.)*
    - ☐ Not all that important because I like to be with my kids.
    - ☐ Vital for me to be an attentive and responsive parent.
    - ☐ Something I have but would like more of.
    - ☐ Something I can't worry about until my kids are older.
    - ☐ Other.

5. Time for my children to be alone and rest during the day is: *(You may choose more than one answer.)*
    - ☐ Something they get to determine by their own rest cycle.
    - ☐ Something I am flexible about.
    - ☐ Something I insist on whether they need it or not.
    - ☐ A benefit to them as well as me.
    - ☐ Other.

6. If my child refuses to take a nap: *(You may choose more than one answer.)*

    ❏ I would insist that he or she do so.

    ❏ I wouldn't care as long as he or she went to sleep easily at night.

    ❏ I would just make bedtime earlier.

    ❏ I would insist on quiet time at least.

    ❏ Other.

7. When my child has refused to take a nap in the past, I have tried these three things that were helpful:

8. When my child has refused to take a nap in the past, three things I have tried that were not so helpful were:

9. After sharing my concerns with others, the next time my toddler refuses to take a nap, I will:

10. Describe your pattern of observing the Sabbath. How do you take breaks during the week?

11. If I were to share the importance of observing the Sabbath with my child, I would say:

12. The strength I gain from Psalm 139:1–3 is:

The eyes of all look to You, and You give
them their food at the proper time.
You open Your hand and satisfy
the desires of every living thing.
(Psalm 145:15–16)

Yuck! I Won't Eat That!

"Where does this food come from?" four-year-old Haley asked her mother. "It comes from the store!" her mother replied. "That's not what Mrs. Juarez, my Sunday school teacher, says! She says all the food we eat comes from God!" Haley said.

It's amazing the truths that come from the mouths of our children. It is God who gives us food to eat, food that causes our preschoolers to grow. They eat to grow physically. And they grow spiritually and emotionally—in faith—from the food that comes from God's Word and sacraments.

But what is a proper nutrition for a toddler or a preschooler? With the number of opinions offered by the medical community, the issue of diet is increasingly confusing. To complicate matters, most children see television commercials that promote food that looks inviting and fun but has little, if any, nutritional value. Our concern for our children's diet and eating habits is a perpetual concern we share with many parents. We worry whether our children are eating too much. We worry whether they are eating enough. We worry that they are not eating a balanced diet.

Perhaps a parent's greatest nutrition fear is that they might harm their children physically and developmentally by not providing the right foods at the right time. On top of that, very few parents have the desire or the time to become short-order cooks to please the whims of their children with individual meals. Every parent prays that their child will grow strong emotionally, physically, and spiritually, and that what they feed their child will enhance that process, not hinder it.

"Give us this day our daily bread." Haley was right: all the food we eat comes from God. As parents, then, we need to continue to let our children know that the food they eat is a gift of God's grace. When we teach our children the Lord's Prayer and its meanings, we do just that. At the same time, we can begin to teach our children that God will help them eat that food for their benefit, then use the energy it gives to love God and our neighbor.

When we eat, we model for our children our participation in the Lord's Supper so they might learn that God refreshes us through the gift of Christ's body and blood. As we do that, we give thanks that God continues to provide for our children's needs, the greatest one being forgiveness of sins.

But I'm not hungry!

My name is Jacki Bates. I live with my husband Greg and our four-year-old daughter Jenna. Jenna is our first child, so I really don't know what is right for a four-year-old's eating habits. I only know that Jenna seems to be going through a phase. When she comes home from preschool, I fix her a snack of milk and cookies or cheese and crackers. Lately, when it comes time for our evening meal, Jenna turns into a person that neither Greg nor I want to be around. Whatever I fix for her, she refuses to eat. One time I fixed hamburgers and French fries, and Jenna's response was, "I hate hamburgers. I'm not hungry."

When she said that, I just calmly said, "Okay, Jenna, what do you want to eat?"

She just replied, "Nothing. I'm not hungry."

Another time we had pizza. Jenna usually loves pizza. But when I put it in front of her, she said, "Yuck, not this pizza! I want to eat at Charley's." Charley's is a pizza emporium in our town.

I've tried a lot of different things. Once I told Jenna I would save her food for her and when she was ready to eat it, I would warm it up. It didn't work. I caught Jenna sneaking some potato chips. I had no idea how long she was eating. All I know is that she ate almost an entire bag.

Another time I told Jenna that she couldn't leave the table until her plate was clean. The only problem was that I got tired of seeing her sitting and moping there. Finally, Jenna gave in and ate her dinner, but it took so long!

My best friend, Cindy, tells me not to worry about it. She says that preschoolers have a way of eating what they need and in the end their diet will not harm them. I'm not as sure about that as Cindy is. In fact, I'm ready to take Jenna to the doctor. If I do, I'm afraid I will learn that I'm a failure as a mother!

I'm not getting much support from Greg. He tells me I'm making too much out of all of this and eventually things will be all right. I wish I could be sure of that, though. I just don't know what to do.

What would you do?

- Jacki said she does not know what is right for a four-year-old to be eating. If you were Jacki, where would you find more information about your child's nutritional needs?

- There is some information we do not know about the Bates's eating habits. We do not know when they eat their evening meal, nor are we aware of any routines associated with their meals. How might time and routines affect Jenna's desire to eat what Jacki or Greg prepare?

- We also have no information about what Jenna does between snack time and the evening meal. How might her play habits or playmates affect her appetite? How would it help Jacki if she kept a closer track of Jenna's activities?

- Jacki has tried different approaches to encourage Jenna to eat. She has tried to fix things she thinks Jenna likes. She has made Jenna sit at the table until she has eaten her meal. What other approaches might Jacki try?

- Cindy told Jacki not to worry about Jenna. In what ways would you agree with Cindy's advice? In what ways would you disagree?

- Could Jenna be saying more to her parents than just, "I don't want to eat the food you have prepared?" What else could Jenna be trying to communicate?

- Finally, Jacki said she is not getting much support from Greg. If you were Jacki, what support would you want from Greg? If you were Greg, what support do you believe you could give?

As loving, caring parents, we are rightfully concerned about our children's diets. We pay attention to the amount and types of food they eat. Both the amount and the nutritional value of food they consume can affect them as they begin to set the pattern for living as adults.

At the same time, we need to be aware that as our children grow, there will be issues over which they struggle with us and confront us. Sometimes the struggle and the confrontation are much more important than the issues themselves. In other words, the more our children grow, the more they will assert their desire to be independent from us. Often the struggle over eating, especially with toddlers and preschoolers, is an attempt to assert their individuality by testing boundaries we have set for them and the limits of our patience. The challenge for parents is to discern the meaning of their behavior and what they are trying to communicate as we continue to travel the often rocky road of parenthood.

As we travel that road, we can trust that God will give us wisdom along every step. We pray for wisdom to discern between a struggle for independence and a developing nutritional habit about which we need to be concerned.

God gives. We receive and give thanks. It is important to reinforce for our children that our food comes from God. We can do that by setting the routine of saying a table prayer that offers thanks to God before every meal. Psalm 145:15 is an excellent prayer to teach your children to use before meals. And, as they grow older, we can encourage our children to lead the family in mealtime prayer.

Our concern about our child's eating habits can be reinforced by our trust that as our child grows physically, she will continue to grow in grace and the knowledge of her Lord and Savior, Jesus Christ. That growth is never-ending, not only for our children but for us as well. Together, we grow in understanding and trust in what God has already given to us in our Baptism. As we celebrate that growth, may we remember that it is God who clothes them. He feeds them. And He sustains them. In the midst of all the challenges and opportunities that parenting provides, our Father in heaven will continue to provide our children and us with all the sustenance we need. As the psalmist writes: "O give thanks to the LORD for He is good and His mercy endures forever." (A good prayer for returning thanks after a meal.)

Closing Prayer

Gracious God, You have created us and You sustain us by giving us what we need to support our bodies and souls. Continue to give my children the food they need so they may grow strong both in body and in faith in You, for Jesus' sake. Amen.

Parent Pairs

How do I know that my child is getting the food she needs? How can I be sure the food she eats truly is the best for her proper growth and nutrition? What do I do when there always seems to be a power struggle when it comes to my child's eating habits?

Read Psalm 145:15–16 and consider the following questions as you discuss the **Parent Pairs** section with your spouse or with another parent.

Yuck! I Won't Eat That!

(To be done with your spouse or another parent.)

1. When it comes to my child's diet, I think: *(Rank in order of importance with #1 being the most important, then #2, #3, etc.)*

   —— I need to be more consistent.

   —— I need to monitor the diet very closely because how my child eats now will influence her eating patterns as she gets older.

   —— I want my child to eat only healthy foods.

   —— I need to be flexible enough to realize that my child's tastes and moods may change daily.

   —— I need to plan my child's afternoon snack early enough so I know my child will be hungry for the evening meal.

   —— I need to be aware of other things that might be going on in my child's life that would cause a change in my child's appetite or eating habits.

   —— I need to recognize that more often than not, this is my child's way of expressing a desire to be an individual who is independent from me.

   —— Other.

2. If I could change one thing about my child's diet, it would be: *(Rank in order of importance with #1 being the most important, then #2, #3, etc.)*

   —— No snacks between meals.

   —— To cut down on sweets and soda.

   —— To make sure my child eats a balanced diet.

   —— To insist that my child eats a good breakfast.

   —— Nothing. I am perfectly satisfied with the way things are.

   —— Other.

3. If my child refuses to eat what has been prepared: *(Rank in order of importance with #1 being the most important, then #2, #3, etc.)*

   —— I should prepare what my child wants to eat.

   —— I would save the meal until my child is ready to eat it.

   —— I would ask what my child had eaten before the meal.

   —— I would make my child remain at the table until the meal was eaten.

   —— I would permit my child to leave the table, thinking that he or she will eat when necessary.

   —— Other.

4. The two ways I would want to teach my child that food is a gift from the heavenly Father are:

5. The prayer we use before our meals is:

6. We always return thanks after we eat.

      Agree   Disagree

7. The prayer we use to return thanks after our meal is:

8. Take some time to help your child write a prayer asking God to bless his food. Also help him write a prayer giving thanks for his food after the meal is completed. Use this space to record these prayers, then share them with other parents.

9. In the past when my child has refused to eat, the two most helpful things I have done were:

10. In the future if my child refuses to eat, the new strategy I want to try is:

11. The strength I gain from Psalm 145:15–16 is:

If your brother sins against you, go and show him
his fault, just between the two of you. If he listens
to you, you have won your brother over. But if he will
not listen, take one or two others along, so that every
matter may be established by the testimony of two
or three witnesses. If he refuses to listen to them,
tell it to the church, treat him as you would a pagan
or a tax collector. I tell you the truth, whatever you
bind on earth will be bound in heaven, and whatever
you loose on earth will be loosed in heaven.
(Matthew 18:15–18)

Mommy, He Hit Me!

In the Bible, God gives the Ten Commandments as
His law for your relationship with Him (Commandments 1–3) and with one another
(Commandments 4–10). When we break them, we sin. During His ministry on earth,
Jesus dedicated a great deal of time to teaching about love, forgiveness, and accountability in caring for and loving one another. For example, in Matthew 18:15–18, Jesus is very
specific by talking about what to do if a brother sins against you.

When we choose a community in which to make our home, we assume that our neighbors will be welcoming and friendly. We expect neighborhood children to receive our
children as playmates. We look carefully at schools, churches, parks, and recreational and
cultural facilities. But sometimes, to our surprise, we move into our dream house or
apartment to find that it is extremely difficult to live with our neighbors.

As adults, we have learned ways of dealing with situations such as these. We learn to
make choices in our relationships. But what is somewhat easy for us is not always easy for
our children. Our children benefit from having friends. When children have friends, they
learn to get along with others. Unfortunately, sometimes our children have difficulty
learning such lessons.

When children become aggressive and argue or fight, sometimes they are trying to tell
us something. Sometimes it is a matter of being selfish and rude. Sometimes they are the
innocent bystanders. Sometimes we struggle with how to best react and how to help our
children learn from such experiences. Often it is hard to figure out who is wrong and who
is right. As Christians, we know that sin is at the bottom of the problem. It is important to
teach our children to repent, to say, "I'm sorry for…". It is also important to teach our children to forgive. This really is living out the baptized life—the daily life of repentance and
forgiveness for all of us, young and old. Finally, sometimes our children learn that not every
child in the neighborhood can be their friend.

The neighborhood bully

My name is Amy Toliver. Jim, my husband, and our four-year-old son, Jared, and I moved into our dream house a few months ago. It's a Victorian-style home that Jim and I have spent the last six months remodeling. It's everything I've ever wanted.

I thought things would be so wonderful here. And they were, until one day when Jared came home with a bloody nose. When I asked how it happened, he didn't say anything at first. I was worried that some other child had done this to him. But when I asked him again, he said that Teddy, a boy who lives across the street, had thrown a ball. Jared missed it and it hit him in the nose. The next week something else happened—Jared came home with a black eye. He looked like he had been through a meat grinder. I finally made Jared talk about it, and he said, "Mommy, he hit me!"

In addition, after Jared comes home from Teddy's house, he uses inappropriate language.

I don't know what to do. I tried to talk to Teddy's parents, but whenever I called, the sitter answered. I tried to talk with Jared about it and he said nothing at all. Jim said that Jared shouldn't play with Teddy anymore. I don't agree. There are no other kids in our neighborhood, and if it weren't for Teddy, Jared would have no one to play with.

I know I'm going to have to do something. Lately Jared has been coming home with more scratches, nicks, and bruises than ever before. I think he's scared of Teddy, even though Teddy is only six months older than Jared.

What do you do when you're afraid your son isn't safe? I want him to be able to protect himself. It's a tough world out there, and I can't always be with him to protect him. I am very much against violence, and I don't want my son growing up thinking he has to fight others to keep safe.

I don't know Teddy's parents. Maybe if I did, this wouldn't be such a crisis. I guess I'll have to keep on trying to communicate with them. Maybe if they knew what was going on, they wouldn't condone it either. All I know is that I want to protect my son, and I wish there were some way all this would stop.

What would you do?

• It appears that Amy and Jim made their decision to buy their home strictly on the home's appearance and its potential to be remodeled. If you were Jim or Amy, what other factors would have influenced your decision? How might you have investigated those factors?

• The first time Jared came home with a bloody nose, he explained that Teddy had thrown the ball and he missed it. If you were Amy, what other questions would you ask Jared about the incident?

• After reading the entire story, it appears that Jared is afraid of Teddy; and he has reason to be. As Jared's parent, what would you say to him that would help him deal with his fears and ensure his safety?

• Amy tried to speak directly with Teddy's parents but was not successful. Let's say Amy finally does meet Teddy's parents. If you were Amy, what would you say to them that would effectively communicate your concerns?

- Amy was frustrated because Jared came home from Teddy's house using inappropriate language. If you were Jared's parent, how would you respond to his using unacceptable language?

- If you were Amy Toliver, to what lengths would you go to protect Jared from Teddy?

- Jim's solution to the problem is to forbid Jared to go to Teddy's house. Amy does not want to do that. What are the other solutions Jim and Amy could explore?

- How might Jared benefit if Amy and Jim included him in their discussion about possible solutions?

Jesus loves everyone. He wants every child to repent and enjoy His forgiveness. What is easy for Jesus to do, however, can be extremely difficult for us to master, especially when our children's safety is at stake. It is hard for us to love the child who is hurting our children. We make any or all attempts to keep our children safe.

When they are not safe, we feel powerless. We feel especially powerless when we are confronted by our own inability to protect our children from anyone who would seek to harm them. As our children grow, it is important to teach them social skills, including ways to resolve conflicts. Our children learn quickly. They will learn from us to bring order and safety into their lives. When we are clear about right and wrong, so will they be. They will learn from that the safety that it brings. They will learn how to choose their friends and thereby protect themselves. They will learn that it is important for parents to talk to other parents to resolve conflict, and that brings order and safety into the community.

As parents, we seek ways to communicate clearly to our children that we will be there for them. When we bring this sense of order and safety into their lives, they translate it as love and concern. The more our children experience this from us, the more successful they will be in resolving conflicts later in their lives. This is how one generation hands down its values and beliefs to the next generation. What is amazing about this process is that we learn about ourselves as well and thereby clarify what we believe.

As we are attentive to the needs and concerns of our children, may we remember how these arguments and conflicts provide the opportunity to teach our children about sin and forgiveness. From them they will learn about their own sin and the sinful world in which they live. Only Christ on the cross was able to make everything right with the Father. Our only hope for fairness is forgiveness through the work of Christ.

Closing Prayer

Gracious God, as my child experiences the stresses and conflicts of childhood, help me to continue to welcome my child and all children and to share Your forgiveness with them. Give me the strength to trust that You will keep my child safe from all harm and danger. In Your Son's name, I pray. Amen.

Parent Pairs

How do parents determine when to let their children solve their conflicts by themselves and when they need help? To what lengths should parents go to ensure the safety of their children? What can parents do to help teach their children effective conflict resolution skills? When is it time to talk to the parents of the other child involved?

Read Matthew 18:15–18 and consider the following questions as you discuss the **Parent Pairs** section with your spouse or with another parent.

Mommy, He Hit Me!

(To be done with your spouse or another parent.)

1. If my child experiences conflicts with other children, I want to be sure that my child: *(Choose as many as may apply.)*

   ❑ Does not initiate violence to resolve conflicts.

   ❑ Does not use violence even if the other child tries to use violence.

   ❑ Is able to come to me so I can help resolve the conflict.

   ❑ Is able to defend himself so bullies won't pick on him.

   ❑ Is able to think of other solutions for resolving the conflict without resorting to violence.

   ❑ Other.

2. As a parent, I think: *(You may choose more than one answer.)*

   ❑ It is important for me to know my children's friends and their parents.

   ❑ It is important to let my children stand on their own two feet and to never intervene.

   ❑ It is not necessary for me to know all my children's friends.

   ❑ It is important for me to set some boundaries with my child and any friends.

   ❑ It is important that my child knows I will be there to support him or her in the midst of any conflict.

   ❑ Other.

3. The best way for me to protect my child from violence is to: *(Choose one.)*

   ❑ Teach my child self-defense skills, such as enrolling him in a class like judo or karate.

   ❑ Try to live in a neighborhood in which incidents of violence are minimal.

   ❑ Create a parent network that would help alert me to any of the issues that concern me.

   ❑ Teach my child effective nonviolent ways to resolve conflict.

   ❑ Teach my child to be street-smart so if she senses physical danger, she will leave the situation as quickly as possible.

   ❑ Other.

4. The most helpful way I have found to encourage my child to deal with fear is to:

5. As a parent, my greatest fear is:

6. My child's greatest fear is:

7. The one conflict I would like to help my child resolve is:

8. My role in the resolution of that conflict should be:

9. If my son or daughter were being bullied by another child, I would:

10. If my child were threatening someone physically, I would:

11. I have talked with my child about what he or she should do when confronted by a bully.

> Agree   Disagree

12. The plan I have developed with my child for dealing with conflict is:

13. I believe it is important to talk with other parents about doing what is possible to stem the tide of violence that afflicts our children.

> Agree   Disagree

14. The strength I gain from Matthew 18:15–18 is:

But just as you excel in everything—
in faith, in speech, in knowledge,
in complete earnestness and in your love
for us—see that you also excel in this
grace of giving.
(2 Corinthians 8:7)

It's Mine!

The book of Acts tells us that after Pentecost the disciples lived together and shared everything in common (Acts 2:44). They were so involved in the ministry of their risen Lord that it made sense for them not to accumulate earthly wealth. In so many respects then, the early followers of Jesus were free from financial burdens and the responsibility of taking care of their property. Everything belonged to God and all was shared with one another. That is why Paul explained in his letter to the Philippians that he had learned that no matter what his financial state, he was content (Philippians 4:11).

Our world is so different from the world of the early Christians. Somehow we have bought into the belief that the more we can hold onto or the more we have, then the more content we will be. However, the seventh commandment, "You shall not steal," and its meaning to protect, defend and improve our neighbor's property remains the same. Sharing is loving your neighbor. In our sinful world, loving our neighbor is difficult, especially if they are not loving toward us. No lessons are ever learned perfectly, but as we grow, and as our preschoolers grow with us, it is God who continues to teach us to grow in understanding the joy that comes with sharing what we have with others.

Part of the challenge of the socialization process is the need for our preschooler to learn that he or she is not the center of the entire universe. In other words, the preschooler is encouraged to discover that she benefits from learning to get along with and play with other preschoolers. It is how they participate in bringing order and love into the community.

In early childhood, a kind of play in which preschoolers commonly engage is playing side by side; a child plays independently but sits next to another. As the preschooler progresses from side-by-side play to interaction with others, the lesson she quickly learns is the importance of sharing. The lesson is often a difficult one. It is sometimes difficult for parents as their children go through it.

Yet as preschoolers progress through some difficult life lessons, we are reminded that God's grace and forgiveness for all of us are new everyday. He will see us through the

77

uncomfortable times. As we journey from one stage to the next, our baptized life teaches us that Jesus worked for forgiveness for the whole world, but He did not keep it. He shares it. He gives it away to those who believe in Him through faith. We are also called to share His forgiveness with our friends.

It's not yours

Johnny, who was three, and Claire, who was four, played together frequently because their mothers, Jill and Jodi, were best friends. Claire was in her second year of preschool and Johnny had just begun preschool. Whenever Jill and Jodi would get together, Johnny and Claire would look at books or play with blocks or cars.

One day, when their mothers were at Jill's house having coffee, Claire discovered that it was great fun playing with Johnny's toy car. Johnny saw how much fun Claire was having. He walked up to her and took the car away from her.

Jill, Johnny's mom, spoke first, "Johnny, Claire was playing with that car. You have to share! Please give it back!"

Johnny shouted, "No, it's my car and she can't have it!"

Claire began to cry and started tugging at the car, "Claire, let go of the car. It's not yours; it really is Johnny's car!" Jodi said.

The tussling continued for a few moments until Johnny gained control of the car. Claire gave up and became interested in some building blocks that were nearby.

Jill said to Jodi, "I really don't know what to do with Johnny! When he doesn't get his nap, he is the most possessive little boy in the entire world! Maybe I should take it as a sign that he is going to grow up to be a very assertive person and will go far!"

When Jodi heard that, she didn't quite know what to say, but she thought, "If Jill thinks Johnny is going to go far in this world, does that mean she thinks poor Claire will be a passive doormat all her life?"

What would you do?

• Jill, Johnny's mom said, "Claire was playing with that car. You have to share! Please give it back!" If you were Jill, how might you have talked with Johnny differently? What would you say to Johnny to explain why it is good to share?

• Claire's mom, Jodi, told her daughter to let go of the toy car. If you were Jodi, how might you have talked with Claire differently?

• The struggle between Johnny and Claire continued until Johnny gained control and Claire became interested in something else. If you were either mother, how could you have intervened to resolve the situation instead of letting Johnny gain control of the car?

• Jill reasoned that Johnny's unwillingness to share was from a lack of sleep caused by not getting a nap. What other reasons might there be for Johnny's unwillingness to share? What other information might be useful to know?

• Jill then turned this struggle for control into an endorsement for Johnny by saying that he would "go far in this world." How helpful was that comment for Jill, Claire, Jodi, or Johnny?

• Jodi heard what Jill said, then thought, "Does she believe Claire will be a passive doormat all her life?" Imagine that you are a friend of Jodi's and she related this incident to you. What would you say to Jodi that might help her deal with this situation in a more positive light for herself and for Claire?

Your child's discovery that he is not the center of the universe can be painful. The first commandment is clear, there is only one God! As parents, patiently correcting our children is important, but it becomes a time to understand sin and grace. Emotions will rise and the struggle will heat up. But remember this is what God called you to do. We need to recognize that often our child's behavior reflects his or her emotions as much as, or more than, needs.

Sharing is never an easy lesson to learn—for adults or preschoolers. But we might help our children learn that lesson more effectively by considering the following:

> • When we have a play date for our child in our home, make sure our child and the playmate have a variety of toys with which they can play.
>
> • Help them initiate play by giving them specific toys to play with.
>
> • Have a timer or a buzzer set to go off to signal time to change toys.
>
> • Communicate to them the boundaries you want them to observe.
>
> • Offer words of encouragement when they successfully demonstrate that they understand what it means to share.
>
> • Model sharing in other areas of your life so your child does not believe that sharing is something that parents expect only children to put into practice.
>
> • Begin to share with your children that God gives us everything, and our grateful response to our Provider is sharing with others.
>
> • Continue to let your children know you love them even when they do not live up to your expectations, such as when it comes to sharing.
>
> • Be aware of opportunities to have the children apologize, i.e., repent and then forgive.

We can tell even very young children that God has blessed us with an abundance of gifts. As we teach this, we can also introduce the concept of stewardship. God calls all His children to be faithful stewards, managers of the myriad gifts He gives. As our children learn to share with others, they are learning to show God's love.

Giving our children the attention and love they need is one way we help them discover God's love for them. It is helping them understand that it is God's grace that draws them into the community of believers. It is God's grace that forgives them when they don't share or when they believe that they are the center of their own universe. As we continue the parenting process, that same grace sustains us, surrounds us, and allows us to rejoice that God continues to love and forgive us as well.

Closing Prayer

O God, I know that the task to which You have called me as a parent is not an easy one. Help me always to see my opportunity to parent as an opportunity to grow in Your grace so that what I do as a parent, I may do to Your glory, now and always, for Jesus' sake. Amen.

Parent Pairs

How do parents teach their children the importance of community? How do parents help their children see beyond themselves and learn the blessings of what it means to share? What can parents do when their children have difficulty learning the art of sharing? How can parents use sharing as a way to explain God's Word and His sacraments?

Read 2 Corinthians 8:7 and consider the following questions as you discuss the **Parent Pairs** section with your spouse or with another parent.

It's Mine!

(To be done with your spouse or another parent.)

1. When my child gets into an argument with a friend or sibling: *(Choose one.)*

   ❏ I intervene only if I can help teach my child something about conflict resolution.

   ❏ I intervene only if my child or the other child is using physical force.

   ❏ I intervene only if my child is not treated fairly.

   ❏ I never intervene because I believe my child has to resolve his own conflicts.

   ❏ Other.

2. When my child plays with another child: *(Choose one.)*

   ❏ I always make sure my child shares.

   ❏ I always make sure both children share equally.

   ❏ I don't worry about sharing; I know the situation will take care of itself.

   ❏ If my child doesn't share, I attempt to interest the other child in another toy or activity.

   ❏ Other.

3. When my child plays with another child: *(Choose one.)*

   ❏ I usually structure their playtime very well with planned activities.

   ❏ I give them plenty of free time.

   ❏ I try to have a balance of free time and structured time.

   ❏ I'm always at their side interacting with them.

   ❏ I leave them alone.

   ❏ Other.

4. My greatest concern when I see my child in a conflict is: *(You may choose more than one answer.)*

   ❏ I worry that my child will harm the other child.

   ❏ I worry that the other child will harm my child.

   ❏ I worry about what the other child's mother will think about me.

   ❏ I worry that I will say something that will shame my child and embarrass me.

   ❏ Other.

5. I try to encourage my child to share by: *(You may choose more than one answer.)*

   ❏ Modeling sharing in my own life.

   ❏ Praising my child when he or she shares.

   ❏ Withholding praise when he or she doesn't share.

   ❏ Distracting my child so he or she might play with something else.

   ❏ Other.

6. I can best teach my child to be a faithful steward by: *(You may choose more than one answer.)*
☐ Telling her about God's love.
☐ Teaching her about how generous it is to share with others.
☐ Telling him about people who would benefit from his sharing.
☐ Talking to her about the underprivileged in this world.
☐ Telling him about how joyful the process of sharing can be.
☐ Other.

7. In the past I have tried the following three ideas to help my child share more easily:

8. When I think of what I have tried, these two ideas have been helpful:

9. When I think of how I have intervened, these two ways have not been helpful:

10. After talking with my friends about sharing, I have decided to try these ideas or strategies:

11. The strength I gain from 2 Corinthians 8:7 is:

But He said to me, "My grace is sufficient for you, for My power is made perfect in weakness." Therefore I will boast all the more gladly about my weaknesses, so that Christ's power may rest on me. (2 Corinthians 12:9)

But I Want It Now!

It is difficult for preschool children to tell the difference between what they need and what they want. After all, especially in our materialistic society, even some adults confuse their wants with their needs. Why should we expect anything less, or more for that matter, from children? Inundated by advertising designed solely to make their parents spend money, children become convinced that their lives will not be complete unless they have a certain toy, play a certain game, or wear a certain article of clothing. If we adults fail to remember at times that God's grace is all we need, why should we be surprised when our children fail to recognize that God provides for all their needs as well?

We acknowledge our sinfulness, but because we continually strive for perfection we tend to want to conceal our weaknesses and imperfections. We become painfully aware of our imperfections when we think they are revealed to others. For instance, when our child has a temper tantrum in a public place, we feel powerless and humiliated—and we feel like a failure as a parent. Many of us just want to hide somewhere until the tantrum passes.

Still, we know that uncontrolled outbursts can happen to any child at any time and are generally no reflection on the parent. It takes a patient and understanding parent to survive them and survive with sanity intact. As they endure the temper tantrum or outburst, both parent and child can learn more about one another as well as learn more about their relationship with our perfect Father.

As we endeavor to come to grips with our imperfection, it is important to remember that we can turn to God and there find continual forgiveness through His Son. Our prayer can be that we grow from the experience of our child's tantrum, to understand ourselves, our child, and, above all, God's perfect love for us. After all, God's mercy truly is everything we need. Anything else comes in a far-distant second to what He has already done for us through Christ. Our faith in Christ gives us the confidence to do what parents need to do to take control and not fear failure. Christ's power to forgive is made perfect in our weakness.

Mommy, why can't I have it?

Caleb was an active three-year-old who was in a hurry to do everything. One day he and his parents, Cal and Geneva, were shopping for a new jacket for Caleb.

Caleb was excited about the new jacket. He knew exactly what he wanted—a new Dashing Dan jacket like his friend Timmy had. Dashing Dan was Caleb's favorite television cartoon character and had become the latest fad with all his friends.

Geneva, knowing fads come and go, decided that Caleb should have a practical jacket he could wear for a longer period of time. Cal didn't have much of an opinion other than he thought Dashing Dan was perhaps the dumbest cartoon character he had ever seen.

With that, the threesome entered the store. Geneva deliberately took Caleb to the section of the store where the Dashing Dan jackets were not to be seen. Caleb asked, "Doesn't this store have Dashing Dan jackets, Mommy?"

Geneva said, "No, Caleb, this store doesn't have Dashing Dan jackets."

So without much fuss, they bought Caleb a brand new green jacket, a practical one that would wear well. Then they made some other purchases in the store. After a half-hour, Geneva had forgotten all about the Dashing Dan section until they walked by it on their way out after checking out.

Caleb's eyes opened wide, "Mommy, Daddy! There's Dashing Dan jackets! Mommy, Daddy can I have one? *Please?*"

"Why Caleb, we just bought you a nice green jacket! You don't need a Dashing Dan jacket!" Cal said.

"But I want it and I want it now!" Caleb cried. Then he threw himself on the floor and began to kick and scream.

As the screaming became more intense, Cal looked at Geneva and said, "Oh, no, here we go again! What do we do now?"

What would you do?

- The clash of wills seems to be set up before Caleb and his parents begin to shop for the jacket. What could Geneva and Cal have done before they went shopping with Caleb to prepare him for their purchase of the jacket?

- Likes and dislikes are important to children. How much should Cal and Geneva have considered Caleb's desire for a Dashing Dan jacket as they took him shopping?

- Geneva deliberately avoided the Dashing Dan section when they entered the store. How might this have contributed to Caleb's uncontrolled outburst as they left?

- Geneva also told Caleb that this store has no Dashing Dan apparel. Rather than say something that wasn't true, what else might Geneva have told Caleb when he asked about Dashing Dan jackets?

- Once Caleb started his uncontrolled outburst, Cal and Geneva react as if they have seen this happen before. What information would you need to help Cal and Geneva try to deal with the situation?

- Cal's reaction—"Oh, no, here we go again! What do we do now?"—seems to indicate that he and Geneva are afraid of Caleb's outburst. What feelings do you think they are experiencing as Caleb kicks and screams? What feelings do you think Caleb is experiencing?

- If you were Geneva and Cal, what would you do now?

A child's uncontrolled outburst is an attempt to communicate more than disappointment and frustration; it is also a child's way of asking his parents to set a boundary or a limit for his behavior. The child who is out of control is asking his parent to take control.

Some ways for parents to be proactive about uncontrolled outbursts are:

- Assess and evaluate their child's history of uncontrolled outbursts.

- Try to find a pattern that emerges from that assessment.

- Analyze any specific areas of stress that lead to the child's tantrums.

- Evaluate the parents' own reaction to that behavior.

- Make a list of possible situations that might cause another uncontrolled outburst.

- Develop a plan to deal with the behavior should an outburst occur.

- Make a commitment to follow through with that plan.

- Communicate clearly to your child in each situation what consequences will happen and what kind of behavior you expect from your child.

- Reward your child with praise when, in a stressful situation, they choose not to act out in an uncontrolled manner.

- Continue to pray to your heavenly Father for wisdom as you deal with your child's uncontrolled outburst.

- Rely on God's grace to know that even good intentions sometimes go awry. The fact that they do does not mean you are a failure as a parent. It does not mean your child is not a good child. Our imperfection and our inability to parent our children in the way we always want are a reflection of the broken and sinful world in which we live.

It takes a caring and a loving parent to take the time to address the issues that cause a child's uncontrolled outbursts. It takes a courageous parent to establish control for his child in the midst of the chaos the child is experiencing. Yet that intervention, in a kind, loving, and consistent way, is exactly what the child needs. It is what God has called you to do as a parent, to bring boundaries, order, and instruction to your child.

Parents are not gods. We must always confess that we do not know everything or see everything. This is why we rejoice in our baptized life, for daily our Lord calls us to repent and enjoy His forgiveness. That forgiveness is available to us as we experience our own unpredictable times of weakness.

Closing Prayer

O God, so often in my life I feel powerless as a parent to control my child in the way I think he or she should be directed. Teach me to depend upon Your power, that in the midst of helpless situations, I know You care for me and for my child through Your love for us in Jesus. In His name, I pray. Amen.

Parent Pairs

How can parents experience God's grace when their child is acting out? How can that child also experience that grace when they are convinced that they not only want every-thing, they *need* everything? How can parents develop an effective plan to deal with their child's temper tantrums?

Read 2 Corinthians 12:9 and consider the following questions as you discuss the **Parent Pairs** section with your spouse or with another parent.

But I Want It Now!

(To be done with your spouse or another parent.)

1. The best way I know how to help my child learn the difference between what he wants and what he needs is:

2. In the midst of a temper tantrum or uncontrolled outburst by my child, I think the most important thing for me to do is: *(Rank in order of importance with #1 being the most important, then #2, #3, etc.)*

   ___ Ignore it completely and hope it will go away.

   ___ Take my child out of the setting if at all possible.

   ___ Leave my child alone, especially if we are at home.

   ___ Be patient, yet firm, as I explain to my child what I expect.

   ___ Try to reason with my child, at the same time asking her what she really wants.

   ___ Give my child an alternative that would help decrease his frustration.

   ___ Other.

3. I think my child's uncontrolled outburst is a way of: *(You may choose more than one answer.)*

   ❏ Wanting to be controlled as soon as possible.

   ❏ Doing bodily what she cannot put into words.

   ❏ Manipulating me into giving him what he wants.

   ❏ Testing me to see how firm I will be.

   ❏ Other.

4. To avoid an uncontrolled outburst by my child, I should: *(You may choose more than one answer.)*

   ❏ Make sure he remembers the last time it happened and what the consequences were.

   ❏ Be thoroughly prepared for any disappointment she may feel and express.

   ❏ Teach my child to express feelings.

   ❏ Give my child more positive reinforcement or attention for good behavior.

   ❏ Other.

5. The most effective way I have of dealing with my child's uncontrolled outbursts is:

6. That way was extremely effective when my child: (*Describe the situation.*)

7. The least effective way I have of dealing with my child's uncontrolled outbursts is:

8. That way was the least effective because my child: (*Describe your child's reaction to your response.*)

9. The one way I would like to change the way I deal with my child's uncontrolled outbursts is:

10. The plan I have for helping my child deal with stressful situations that might cause an uncontrolled outburst is:

11. If I were to give a friend advice about her child's uncontrolled outbursts, I would say:

12. The strength I gain from 2 Corinthians 12:9 is:

"Be still, and know that I am God;
I will be exalted among the nations,
I will be exalted in the earth." The LORD
almighty is with us; the God of Jacob
is our fortress.
(Psalm 46:10–11)

Just Wait, Mom!

We live in a world that insists on instant gratification and constant busyness. We have fast food, automatic teller machines, remote control televisions, microwave ovens, fax machines, the Internet, the list goes on and on. These are all gifts from God. Despite such conveniences, there never seems to be enough time to do everything we think we should do. Interruptions and events rob parents of valuable time that is already in short supply.

Bruce G. Epperly, in his book on spirituality and health, describes the world in which we live as one that has been infected by "hurry sickness." [1] He says that we are driven by pressures to beat the clock. He refers to a study conducted in the early 1960s that predicted that people would have much more leisure time as a result of labor saving devices that would relieve stress. However, the opposite is true. There is more stress and more anxiety than we believed years ago would be the case.[2]

Sometimes we as parents fall into hurry sickness out of love for our children. We want our children to have all of the right experiences in life. Suddenly we are trapped by our schedules! The sickness sets in. "Just wait, Mom!" we hear.

"Be still and know that I am God." Our children do not need every experience that we did not have growing up. God calls us to be parents in order to bring reasonable order into our children's lives. Our call as a parent is often to decide what our children need to do and what we as parents can handle in our daily schedule.

Psalm 46 is the foundation for a great hymn of the church, "A mighty fortress is our God, a trusty shield and weapon; He helps us free from every need that hath us now o'ertaken." As parents we remember that the "LORD almighty is with us; the God of Jacob is our fortress." Sometimes we feel like we need a fortress. We need protection from television, answering machines, soccer practice, piano practice, and the rest of our schedules. Not only does God give us the gifts of creation, our children, and time, but He also gives to us Himself in the sacramental life. There, in His Word and sacraments, does the Lord almighty dwell with us for mercy and forgiveness. There is our fortress of safety.

[1] Bruce G. Epperly, *Spirituality and Health—Health and Spirituality—A New Journey of Spirit, Mind and Body* (Mystic, CT: Twenty Third Publications, 1997), p.45.
[2] Ibid. page 45–46.

But I'm not ready yet!

My name is Marlys McCoy and I'm mother of a girl named Christy. Christy is four-and-a-half years old. She stays with her dad every other weekend during the school year and for an extended period of time during the summer.

I work hard as a nurse on the evening shift. I work hard to be a good mom to Christy. I'm a very busy person, and I'm on a tight schedule. Sometimes I need to shift Christy from here to there—from day care, to a friend's house, to swimming lessons, to dance class.

You might think Christy is too busy for a child her age, but when I grew up, I didn't have the opportunities that I'm trying to give her. My parents were too poor to let me do what I wanted to do. I often dreamed what it would be like to do all the things that Christy is doing. I'm determined to give her the chance to do everything I didn't get to do.

Don't get me wrong. I wouldn't make her do them if she didn't like them. But for now, Christy likes them; at least she says she does. The only problem is, whenever we go anywhere, I have to tell Christy a half dozen or more times to get ready. Then, after I tell her, she still isn't ready. She always says, "Just a minute, Mom!" or "I'm not ready yet!"

I've tried to be patient about all of this, but my patience is running pretty thin. I've tried to give her extra time, but the more time I give her, the more she daydreams and dawdles. Some say I should help her get ready. But there's no way I'm going to do that for her. After all, she's four-and-a-half and next fall she will be starting kindergarten. Then she'll have to know what it's like to get ready on time.

I wish I knew how to solve this. I'm sure you think I'm making a big deal of it. But you're not me, and you don't live the way I do. I'm just trying to do the best I can for Christy and for me.

What would you do?

- As you listen to Marlys tell her story, what concerns do you have for her? for Christy?

- Marlys is determined to give Christy the opportunity to do everything that she did not get to do when she was growing up. How helpful a goal is that for Marlys or for Christy? How realistic is that goal?

- Marlys seems to be waiting for Christy to let her know if she is making her do too much. Is this realistic?

- Might the issue be different or the same for a two-parent home?

- Discuss the different things Christy might be trying to say to her mother when she says, "Just a minute, Mom. I'm not ready yet!"

- How are Marlys and Christy both victims of "hurry sickness"? What might they do to alleviate their situation?

Parents are busy people. We try to do everything we need to do. We try to be the best parents for our children. Sometimes we painfully discover that our schedules and our children's are out of sync. When that happens, we discover that we are not in control—of our schedules or of our children.

As we struggle with impatience and frustration, we need to be aware of our children's needs. We also need to be sensitive to the possibility that they may not want to tell us what they really need; they may be afraid of disappointing us. We need to recognize that their inability to stay on task may mean a variety of things, including their inability to understand time. As we address their needs, we can pray for patience and discernment. Hopefully, we can acknowledge what it is they are trying to say about us, about their own frustration, and about their ability to adapt to the pressure of the hectic pace we often ask of them.

These situations can encourage us to look at our own values. Do we over-program our children when, in fact, what they truly want from us is not one more activity but simply our presence? They crave spending time with us, having our attention. Are we teaching our children to be involved in everything and be committed to everything? Maybe our own children are leading us to understand that to be committed to everything is, in reality, to be committed to nothing.

Throughout it all, the Lord God remains patient with us even when we are not patient with our children. Ultimately, through these precious children, God invites us to rely on Him as our source of faith, strength, and peace. He calls us weekly to His fortress to feed, strengthen, and forgive us. From church on Sunday to our daily schedule, the Lord brings focus and priority. From daily repentance and forgiveness we better understand what is important in our schedules, especially time with our children. "The LORD almighty is with us; the God of Jacob is our fortress."

Closing Prayer

Dear God, as I struggle with my busy schedule and my attempts to juggle all the responsibilities I've assumed, help me to be still and rely on You as I deal with my child. Give me the serenity to know the gift of Your peace that You have given me through Jesus Christ, my Lord and Savior. Draw me closer to You as I hear Your Word and enjoy Your sacraments. In Jesus' name. Amen.

Parent Pairs

How do we decide what activities our children participate in? How can we manage our schedules and commitments, especially time with our children and with God? How can we learn from our children to sharpen our focus on our heavenly Father as the source of our faith and life? How can we bring reasonable order to our schedule and our child's schedule?

Read Psalm 46:10–11 and consider the following questions as you discuss the **Parent Pairs** section with your spouse or with another parent.

Just Wait, Mom!

(To be done with your spouse or another parent.)
1. List the activities that reflect a typical day in your life as a parent.

2. When I look at my daily schedule, I believe: *(Choose one.)*
   - ☐ Although I am doing too much, there is nothing I could change.
   - ☐ I am comfortable with the balance in my life between home, church, work, and family.
   - ☐ I wish I could tear it up and start over again.
   - ☐ I think there are some things that need readjusting.
   - ☐ Other.

3. As I look at my daily schedule, the thing I value most according to my commitment of time is:

4. When I look at the time demands on my children: *(Choose one.)*
   - ☐ I am comfortable that their schedules are manageable.
   - ☐ It's no wonder they don't come when I tell them to.
   - ☐ I think I am demanding too much from them.
   - ☐ I need to sort out what is important for them to do and why.
   - ☐ Other.

5. When I look at my child's life and the activities he is committed to, the thing I am trying to teach him to value the most is:

6. To emphasize my commitment to God and my child's commitment to God, I can change:

7. When my child tells me to "just wait": *(Choose one.)*
   - ☐ I count to 10, and then start all over again.
   - ☐ I demand a proper response instantly.
   - ☐ I know my child needs more attention from me.
   - ☐ I realize this is my child's way of paying me back for all the times I've made him wait.
   - ☐ Other.

8. Some of the things I have tried in the past when my child has responded slowly to what I wanted are:

9. As I look at the things I have done when I have tried to address the problem, these three were most helpful:

10. As I look at the things I have tried, the following two were least helpful:

11. If I could change my schedule, I would:

12. If I could change my child's schedule, I would:

13. After talking with others, my plan to deal with my child's procrastination is:

14. The strength I derive from Psalm 46:10–11 is:

After three days they found Him in the
temple courts, sitting among the teachers,
listening to them and asking questions.
Everyone who heard Him was amazed
at His understanding and His answers.
(Luke 2:46–47)

How My Child Compares to Others

It is an undeniable fact of life: parents love to talk about
their children, especially when their children do something well. Pride is an expected out-
come of the parenting process. After all, being a parent is hard work. The rewards can be few
and far between. So when little Billy or little Jenny does something that pleases their parents,
most parents take time to share their pleasure with their children and with others as well.

Sometimes, however, those who listen to endless stories about Billy or Jenny may wonder, "Why can't my child be like those children? Why are their children more advanced
than my son or daughter? What am I doing wrong?" The more parents worry about their
own parenting skills and their child's accomplishments, the less inclined they are to listen
when other parents want to share.

A fascinating possibility about the Bible story from which the above verses are taken is
that Joseph and Mary may have asked themselves the same question other parents have:
"Why can't our son be more like other children?"

The family—Joseph, Mary, and Jesus—was returning from an important Jewish festival in
Jerusalem. They were traveling with a large group of relatives and acquaintances. Mary may
have assumed that 12-year-old Jesus was with Joseph; or perhaps Joseph assumed Jesus was
with His mother. Regardless, when the discovery is made, Mary and Joseph immediately
retraced their journey all the way to Jerusalem. How did they feel? We can only wonder about
the conversation during their three-day search for their son. We do know that they found Him
in the temple, teaching the teachers themselves.

Mary responded in a typical parental way: "Son, what are you doing? Don't you know that
your father and I have been worried sick about you? Why are you treating us this way?" Jesus'
answer was not expected; nor would typical parents consider it to be acceptable. However,
Jesus reminded Mary that He was doing the work of His Father, His heavenly Father.

As we realize what took place here, we can appreciate Mary and Joseph's situation. We
can recognize that even the human parents of the divine Son of God may have had ups and

downs. We can learn from Joseph and Mary that we can appreciate and cherish each moment God gives us with our children. We can discover the joys of accepting our children for the people God has created them to be. Finally, appreciating the gift of God's creation through our children, we can learn that our children need only measure up to God and not other children. They measure up to God only through faith in Christ. By God's grace, our children can learn many things. They need to do their best and work hard. However, it is all done under our children's umbrella of Baptism. Like us they must live their lives, and learn to trust God—He provides daily bread and heavenly food.

I'm so proud!

My name is Tanya. I'm the mother of two. Terry, my boy, is six, and Erica, my girl, is two. I love my children, and I am proud of them. But let's face it, my children have never been kids that anyone would notice at first glance. They're good kids. They never cause any trouble. But they never have been superstars either. They'll be okay in life, at least I hope. Terry took his time learning to walk. He didn't say much until he was almost three-and-a-half. Erica walked early, but she's following in her brother's footsteps when it comes to talking.

I think I could live with all of this if it weren't for my friends. Whenever I'm with my friends, they always talk about their kids, and, honestly, you'd think all of them have geniuses for children. I have one friend whose four-year-old knows how to read and counts to 100. I have another friend with a daughter who was toilet trained at 15 months. And another friend thinks her son does nothing wrong. Whenever our kids play together, her son always blames Erica or Terry for anything that happens and, to make matters worse, his mother believes him. Do they really think their children are perfect?

Whenever I see my friends or their children, I begin to wonder if there is something wrong with my kids. More to the point, I think there's something wrong with me, the genes I gave my kids, and the way I parent them. Sometimes I think if I were a better parent, Erica and Terry would know how to do more. I often wonder if I'm doing enough for them. The trouble is, I just don't have enough time. You see, I work extra hours each week just to make ends meet. So when I come home at night, after I have picked up Erica and Terry at my mother's house, I don't have much time or energy left to work with them.

It's getting to the point that I don't want to see my friends anymore. If I tell them I don't want to hear about their children because I think there are other things to talk about, I'm afraid they won't want me as a friend. I'm just as proud of my kids as my friends are of theirs, and I wish there was a way for me to tell them that. Yet I wonder why the grass always seems greener on the other side of the fence.

What would you do?

- Tanya presents the issue as a single parent. How would the perspective change or be the same if the parents were together?

- If you were a friend of Tanya, what would you tell her so she would be less affected by what others say?

- Tanya says that if she were a better parent, things might be different with Erica and Terry. If you agree, what could Tanya be doing differently? If you disagree, what could Tanya do that would help her feel better about her parenting abilities?

• Tanya wonders if she should tell her friends how she feels when they talk about their children. Why might you agree? If you were Tanya, what would you say to your friends when they talk about their children?

• It seems as though Tanya's time with her friends who talk about their children leads her to identify feelings of inadequacy in terms of her effectiveness as a mother. What could Tanya do to help her understand or deal with these feelings?

• Tanya says that she's not sure whether she wants to see her friends anymore, especially if they talk about their children. What other options might Tanya choose?

We often let other people define our feelings and control our emotions and attitudes, especially when it comes to how we feel about our children. Sometimes, when we hear other parents singing the praises of their children, we let feelings of guilt and shame surface about the way we parent or we try to compete on their level and counter their children's accomplishments with those of our own children.

As we encounter trying times like these, it might be helpful for us to:

• *Have a network of friends we trust whom we can talk with about our parenting concerns.* It is good to have a network of Christian friends who know us and accept us. At the same time, we can trust that they won't make us feel ashamed of the way we parent.

• *Focus on our children and their own uniqueness.* As we do that, we can recognize that they are individuals whom God created. They are God's gifts to us. They have their own talents (as well as peculiarities). Through Baptism, God has adopted all of us into His family to be His faithful servants. As members of the body of Christ, we know that each of God's children has been called to continue His mission and His work and to receive fully His grace, mercy, and love in Christ Jesus.

• *Remember that God calls us to be parents.* As such, that means we have entered into a holy vocation. He has set us apart for the expressed purpose of parenting the children He entrusts to us, whether through birth or adoption. Since God has called us to be parents, He will empower us to be faithful to that calling and will equip us for the role through family, friends, and others.

• *Remember that we are baptized, chosen, and forgiven parents.* We do realize and confess that we sin and are not perfect parents. God forgives us and thereby grants us the confidence to wake up and parent all over again tomorrow. We do our best and enjoy His grace. We thank Him for others who help us learn to be parents.

As we consider our calling as parents, we can remember that our children will develop at a unique rate, not necessarily on schedule or in the same way as other children their age. Acknowledging this, we can see our children for who they are, in their own right and in their own way. We value them for who they are rather than trying to compare or contrast them with other children.

The more our children grow, the more we can rejoice in their individuality, people who are separate from us and who are baptized and redeemed members of the body of Christ. As our children grow, may our appreciation of their unique gifts grow with them. Thank God for the blessings those gifts bring to us and to His kingdom.

Closing Prayer

O Lord God, You have blessed me with the precious gift of my child. Yet so often I am tempted to focus on what my child cannot do instead of being thankful for what my child can do. Help me to accept and love my child totally and completely, as you continue to accept and love me through Christ's love and sacrifice. In His name. Amen.

Parent Pairs

How can I focus on always being thankful for the gift of my child rather than on the accomplishments of other children? What can I do when other parents continually talk about their children and I find that I feel inadequate?

Read Luke 2:46–47 and consider the following questions as you discuss the **Parent Pairs** section with your spouse or with another parent.

How My Child Compares to Others

(To be done with your spouse or another parent.)

1. The three friends I can talk with about my parenting skills who do not allow me to feel guilty or inadequate about those skills are:

2. If I could give someone one encouraging piece of advice about feeling confident about parenting, it would be:

3. The fact that God has called me to be a parent helps me:

4. The fact that God has called me to be His child in Baptism helps me:

5. When my friends talk about their children, I: *(Choose one.)*
   - ❏ Tell outrageous stories about my children just to make them jealous.
   - ❏ Listen very politely, yet at the same time, wish they would talk about something else.
   - ❏ Try to change the subject.
   - ❏ Try to show how happy I am for them because I would want them to react in the same way about my children.
   - ❏ Other.

6. When people say great things about their children and not mine, I: *(You may choose more than one answer.)*

   ❑ Wonder what I have done to have children who seem to be so uninteresting.

   ❑ Think that I am not a very good parent.

   ❑ Think about finding different friends.

   ❑ Ignore it.

   ❑ Other.

7. The most important thing I can do for my children when I am with my friends is: *(Choose one.)*

   ❑ Not to think less of them because I think my friends' children have accomplished more.

   ❑ Concentrate on the unique capabilities of my children.

   ❑ Keep telling myself I am a good parent.

   ❑ Try to learn something from my friends' parenting skills rather than be defensive about my own.

   ❑ Other.

8. Write five positive characteristics you have as a parent. Keep that list where you can find it and read it daily.

9. Write five positive characteristics your children possess. Refer to it daily.

10. When I feel inadequate as a parent because other parents have praised their children incessantly, I need to: *(Check all that apply.)*

    ❑ Focus on the positive traits my children possess.

    ❑ Ignore them because they have no power over me.

    ❑ Remind myself that they are feeling inadequate about themselves or they wouldn't need to praise their children so much.

    ❑ Make a mental note to contact the people who surround me with unconditional love.

    ❑ Try to change the subject.

    ❑ Make sure I don't talk to these parents for a long time.

    ❑ Be happy that they are undoubtedly proud of their children.

    ❑ Other.

11. The strength I receive from Luke 2:46–47 is:

But the fruit of the Spirit is love, joy, peace, patience, kindness, goodness, faithfulness, gentleness and self-control. Against such things there is no law.
(Galatians 5:22–23)

Diapers Forever

"Be patient, God isn't finished with me yet!" is a sentiment that has been used to encourage adults, especially parents, to be understanding with children. Parents can be in a hurry to see progress and believe that if their child isn't on schedule like everyone else's child, then something is wrong.

Patience is a virtue, but we find it very difficult to be patient, especially when it comes to toilet training our toddler or preschooler. Often fraught with anxiety and struggle, it can either be a painful process or a journey in which both child and parent discover new and important things about one another. Parents can discover their own level of tolerance as well as their ability to deal with the inevitable messes toilet training brings. And children can take joy in accomplishing a significant goal and find satisfaction in being more grown up.

As you approach each opportunity to toilet train your child, it might be helpful for you to:

- Remember that your child is unique. It does not help you or your child to compare her to an older sibling or to little Susie next door. Each child approaches the undertaking in his or her unique way.

- Make sure you plan toilet training to coincide with a period in your family's life when there is time and opportunity to stay on task and focus on the goal. Choose a time, if possible, when there is a minimal amount of stress in your life. It is extremely counterproductive to use toilet training as an excuse to add to your stress or the stress of your child.

- Be patient. Very few children catch on in a quick or decisive way.

Certainly, this chapter is not an attempt to contribute to the massive amount of advice on the subject of toilet training. It is, however, your opportunity to share with one another your strategies, concerns, and joys as you train your child. In a sense, it is also recognition that as we train our children, they train us and help us adjust to each new phase they achieve. As you share goals, hopes, and dreams, even in the midst of tasks that are unpleasant, remember that even as adults we continue to grow and reach new phases. We can share our confidence and faith that God's goal of making us His own has been accomplished through water and His Word. Since He has adopted our children and us into His family, we can press on with all the related tasks of parenting—even toilet training—and at the same time, thank God that He gives us the opportunity to do so.

How long can this go on?

Hi! My name is Karen. Rick and I are the parents of a boy, six years old, named Jacob, and a girl, Jessica, almost three. When Jacob was Jessica's age, it seemed like we had more time. It was a wonder to see him grow. And it seemed like he handled every stage with ease. He went through the teething stage without being crabby. By 14 months, he was completely toilet trained. I could put training pants on him when he went to bed at night. When he woke in the morning, they would be completely dry.

I had listened to all the horror stories from my friends about their children. But I never realized that it could be that bad—until Jessica was born, that is. It seems like every stage has been a struggle for Jessica. When she was eight months old, we still were getting up once a night. As she's gotten new teeth, she's made sure that we all know the intensity of her discomfort.

My problem—actually it's Jessica's problem—is that toilet training does not interest her at all. I mean, it's not as if I expect her to be Jacob. When she was 14 months old, I didn't even try to train her. But now that she's almost three, I think it's about time.

So, for a time each day, I'd ask her if she wanted to be like a "big girl" and wear panties. For at least two hours each day, she'd wear them. I'd place her on the potty chair before we put them on, and place her back on the potty chair after the time period. And once in between, I'd do the same thing. Nothing happened. Except usually when I'd put her diaper on, she would do what I had hoped she would do in the toilet.

I've tried other things. I've tried rewards. I've tried incentives. I figured I could even do better if I gave her a doll and had her toilet train the doll. But I think I'm at my wit's end. How long can this go on? I'm tired of cleaning up messy pants, messy floors, and messy bottoms. I'm almost to the point of saying, "It'll never happen, will it?"

Maybe all of this is my punishment for telling everyone how good Jacob was when he was a baby and what kind of superstar he was. Because I did that, I doubt that anyone wants to hear about my struggles. Or perhaps everyone would so they could say, "See, I told you so!" I'm feeling alone in this struggle, and I don't think I can talk to anyone.

What would you do?

- Karen said that because Jacob was the first, she and Rick had more time for him. How could spending more time with your son or daughter affect the toilet-training process?

- How did Karen let her experience with Jacob set her up to be disappointed as Jessica moved through those same phases?

- Karen referred to the horror stories she'd heard about children and how she did not realize things could be that bad until Jessica was born. How helpful is it for Karen to use words like "bad" and "horror" when describing her experience with Jessica? What other words might be more helpful for Karen to use?

- Who has the problem here, and what can Jessica or Karen do about solving it?

- Karen has said she has tried everything. If you were Karen, what would your next move be?

- Karen seems embarrassed and thinks she's alone in this process. What reasons would you give Karen about why it is important that she share her concerns with her friends?

- We never hear about Rick's input in this process. How might Rick play a helpful role in toilet training?

If at first you don't succeed, try, try again. The words are especially true when it comes to toilet training. When we put a great deal of pressure on our children to succeed, we place a great deal of pressure on ourselves as well. When our children fail, we sometimes interpret it as though we ourselves have failed. We think we need to do better. When we forget that, we fall into the trap of thinking that we are dependent on what we can accomplish ourselves.

What counts as we proceed with any aspect of parenting, including toilet training, is not *our* success or failure, but whether our children gain a sense of accomplishment and fulfillment by achieving another stage in their lives. For us to help them progress, we need to remember that timing is key. Some children are ready to be toilet trained at a much younger age than others. We also need to be aware that the process may take longer for some children than others. Finally, we should keep in mind that the readiness and the length of the learning process are not a reflection of our abilities as parents or of the intelligence of our children. Our own sense of accomplishment and fulfillment need not be tied to our children's accomplishments. At the same time, our children's feelings of self-worth and self-esteem ought not be tied to their ability to accomplish a task in order to meet our expectations or our schedule.

Again, as we find ourselves caught up with our children's accomplishments, or lack of them, we are surrounded by God's grace. Because of this, we can reassure our children that whenever they fail to reach a goal or meet expectations (their own or someone else's), God's grace for them as His baptized and redeemed children never fails. As Christians we never pretend there is anything we do, deed, goal, or accomplishment, that does not need God's mercy and grace. We live fully in that grace, and because of it we can give thanks to God for all the opportunities He gives us as parents—even the opportunity to toilet train our children.

Closing Prayer

Loving God, help me to set realistic goals for my child and for myself as a parent. As I strive to reach these goals, help me remember that You love me and You love my child. Through Jesus Christ, Your Son, You have made my child and me Your own children. Help me live as Your child now and always, for Jesus' sake! Amen.

Parent Pairs

What are my expectations for my child during the toilet training process? What do I expect of myself? How do I know when my child is ready for toilet training? What are my views and beliefs about the subject? If I feel frustrated by the process, with whom would I share my frustrations?

Read Galatians 5:22–23 and consider the following questions as you discuss the **Parent Pairs** section with your spouse or with another parent.

Diapers Forever

(To be done with your spouse or another parent.)

1. When it comes to toilet training, I believe the more attention I give my child, the more quickly he or she will be trained.

      Agree   Disagree

2. Children who are not firstborn children are more difficult to toilet train.

      Agree   Disagree

3. There is one effective, foolproof method for toilet training a child.

      Agree   Disagree

4. When it comes to toilet training, I think: *(Rank in order of importance with #1 being the most important, then #2, #3, etc.)*

    ——Consistency is the key.

    ——Timing is everything because no child will be toilet trained until he or she is ready.

    ——Patience is a virtue because children who are being toilet trained can never be hurried.

    ——Parents need to be flexible.

    ——Parents need to be firm.

    ——Parents need to treat toilet training as if it were one great, exciting adventure.

    ——Parents need to talk about it with other respected adults.

    ——Other.

5. I praise my child: *(Check one.)*

    ❏ Always.

    ❏ Sometimes.

    ❏ Not as much as I should.

    ❏ I'm usually more critical.

6. When it comes to toilet training, I should: *(You may choose more than one answer.)*

    ❏ Be more patient.

    ❏ Be more persistent.

    ❏ Praise my child more.

    ❏ Praise my child only when he or she does what I want them to do.

    ❏ Be more kind and caring.

    ❏ Not worry so much.

7. If I were to talk with someone about the joys and frustrations of toilet training, I would say:

8. I would talk to that person because:

9. Two strategies I have used in toilet training my children that have been extremely helpful are:

10. Two strategies I have used in toilet training my children that have not been helpful are:

11. The differences between the strategies that were helpful and the strategies that were not helpful are:

12. If I were to give helpful advice about toilet training to another parent and summarize it in one sentence, it would be:

13. The strength I gain from Galatians 5:22–23 is:

On the eighth day, when it was time
to circumcise Him, He was named Jesus,
the name the angel had given Him
before He had been conceived.
(Luke 2:21)

The Birthday Bash

Birthdays are important milestones in the lives of our children. They are important milestones in our lives as parents as well. It makes no difference whether we are birth parents or adoptive parents. We want our children to know that they are gifts from God! We want them to know how thankful we are that God called us to be their parents. We truly celebrate the blessings that they are to us, and we pray that they continue to be a blessing to all people.

Celebrations were important in Jesus' day. For example, when a male child was circumcised, he was given a name. Circumcision marked him as a chosen one, a member of the children of Israel.

For the same reasons, birthdays and Baptism anniversaries are a time of joy today, especially for little ones. We joyously celebrate our children's conception, birth, and Baptism, for they all mark a new gift, a new beginning, and a new life.

How parents choose to celebrate these important milestones is an important decision for establishing family traditions. The way we choose to celebrate reflects our values as well as our faith. Oftentimes we are distracted by the logistics and lose the sense for why we celebrate the milestones. We can become so "wrapped" up in the presents and the trappings that we lose the reason for the celebrations themselves. We risk focusing on the gifts rather than giving thanks to God for the gifts He gives in creation and Baptism.

Perhaps this is easier said than done. We are vulnerable to wanting our children's parties to be like every other child's party. If our friends or relatives give their child an elaborate birthday party, we feel the pressure to do the same. If our son or daughter attends another child's party, we feel obligated to invite that child to our child's party. Unfortunately, even as we celebrate these wonderful milestones, competition and obligation can dominate the day.

A mother at a parenting workshop was asked to complete this sentence: "The purpose of celebrating my child's birthday is to. …" "Purpose" is where we should start. God co-creates in conception with parents. He recreates in Baptism! Maybe that's where we should begin as we celebrate their birthdays and their lives.

We're having how many *kids?*

Deb was excited. Her daughter, Tally, was turning four in another month and she was busy planning her birthday party. As Deb planned whom she would invite, she made a list. First, there were the children who had invited Tally to their birthday parties over the last year. Since they had invited Tally, they deserved an invitation to Tally's party in return.

Next there were those children Deb thought Tally should get to know. Deb had met their parents at preschool and thought, "I wish Tally would get to know these children better! In fact, I wish I could get to know these parents better. They really seem like fun people to know."

Finally, there were the invitations that Deb considered politically correct, those children she felt they had to invite or she or her husband Don would face the consequences. There was Chad, Don's nephew, whom they rarely saw. If Deb didn't invite Chad to Tally's party, Don's parents would be upset. Then there was Marsha's girl, Samantha. Deb hadn't seen Marsha in almost a year, but the last time Deb had seen her, she remarked that Samantha was looking forward to going to Tally's birthday party.

That night when both Deb and Don came home from work, Deb began the conversation by saying, "I have Tally's birthday party pretty well planned! I think we will go to Bucky Beaver's Pizza Emporium, and then we will come here for a few games and the cake."

"That sounds great!" Don optimistically replied. "By the way, how many kids are we inviting to this fantastic event?"

Deb cautiously cleared her throat, and said "By my last count, 15!"

"We're having *how many?* Did you say 15? I fail to see why Tally needs *15* kids at her birthday party. She won't remember a year from now if she had five or 15 there. Do you have any idea how much this extravaganza will cost?"

"You just don't understand, Don!" Deb replied as she was close to tears.

What would you do?

• As Deb goes down her guest list, she includes those children who have invited Tally to their birthday parties. If you were Deb, what reasons would you give for inviting them? What reasons would you give for not inviting them?

• Next, Deb includes the children whose parents she would like to get to know. What other ways could she get to know these people other than using Tally's birthday party as the icebreaker?

• Finally, she includes the politically correct guests, the children she feels obligated to invite. What reasons would you give for not inviting those children?

• Don makes the comment that a year from now Tally won't remember how many children came to her birthday party. If you were Don, what would you say to Deb that you would want Tally to remember about her birthday party?

• As we read the story, it appears as though Don has had no part in planning the birthday party. What role do you believe Don should play in the planning?

• Also, nowhere in the story are we given any clue that Deb has sought input from the guest of honor, Tally. What role should a four-year-old play in planning her own birthday party?

- Don's final argument against having so many children at Tally's birthday party is that it will be expensive. If you were Deb, how would you respond to Don's concern?

- Deb's response to this is, "You just don't understand!" If you were Deb, what would you say to Don that would help him understand?

- Deb's discussion is all about Tally. She is missing an opportunity to talk about whom?

Milestones create memories, establish traditions, and are the vehicles to hand down the Christian faith. Milestones help form our children's future values. Finally, milestones are building blocks in the foundation upon which our children move to the next stage in their life journey. As parents, we need to take the time to understand the milestones the church provides to help him or her continue on their baptismal journey. How will the birthday milestone help a child learn more about God's creation? A birthday is an opportunity to teach a child that God works through that creation. God co-creates a child with parents. In turn, the child is raised in his or her Baptism and learns to become a good neighbor who not only brings love to the community, but also can bring mercy and forgiveness through Christ.

Birthday milestones are wonderful events for families. They are times when friends, neighbors, and relatives gather to celebrate their family. Birthdays are also times for families to hand down their values, standards, and traditions for family celebrations, a time to hand down what they believe.

Interestingly, for many families, values, concerns, and expectations vary widely between the members of the family. Family members need to communicate clearly their expectations about such celebrations. The more proactive families are at talking about the meaning of celebrations, the more significant those celebrations will be to the family.

May our celebrations reflect faith in God as the Giver of every good, perfect, and joyous gift. May God grant us the grace to hand down to our children the two-fold gifts that birthday celebrations bring our child—a gift in creation and gifts in Baptism. God called us to teach our child to take these gift to the world.

Closing Prayer

O God, as I look forward with joy and anticipation to birthday milestones in the life of my child, help me to remember every day that my child is a unique and precious gift You have given to me. Thank You for Your gift, O God. Amen.

Parent Pairs

What is the goal and purpose of the birthday celebration I plan for my child? What do I want to teach my child about God as we celebrate my child's birthday? How will the kind of party I give and the people in attendance reflect the community of faith of which our family is a part?

Read Luke 2:21 and consider the following questions as you discuss the **Parent Pairs** section with your spouse or with another parent.

The Birthday Bash

(To be done with your spouse or another parent.)

1. My most memorable birthday as a child was: *(Describe the occasion.)*

2. My least favorite birthday as a child was: *(Describe the occasion.)*

3. I want my child's birthdays to be similar to the kinds of birthdays I celebrated as a child in the following three ways:

4. I want my child's birthdays to be different from the kinds of birthdays I celebrated as a child in the following three ways:

5. I think that as birthday milestones are celebrated in the lives of children, it is important to: *(Rank in order of importance with #1 being the most important, then #2, #3, etc.)*

____Consider the cost when planning the party.

____Do what I can as a parent to create a lasting memory for my child.

____Teach my child about her new birth in Baptism.

____Include the birthday child in deciding how his or her birthday will be celebrated.

____Make sure no one will be offended if they are left off the invitation list.

____Place the emphasis on the celebration and not on the gifts received as part of that celebration.

____Create such a fun party that the children who attend will wish to return.

____Go over budget once in a while.

____Other.

6. The purpose of celebrating my child's birthday is to: *(Choose one.)*
   - ❏ Help my child find new friends.
   - ❏ Get gifts for my child.
   - ❏ Teach my child about God's gifts of life in conception and birth.
   - ❏ Help my child mature in socialization skills.
   - ❏ Have an excuse to invite friends and relatives to my home.
   - ❏ Other.

7. If I could arrange the perfect birthday party for my child without worrying about the cost, I would do these three things:

8. Within my budget constraints, the party I would arrange for my child would be:

9. The kind of party my child would want would be:

10. The size and the kind of birthday parties for children should differ according to age.

    Agree   Disagree

11. My child's baptismal date is:

12. My prayer for my child as I plan his or her birthday party is:

13. The strength I gain from Luke 2:21 is:

Train a child in the way he should go, and when he is old he will not turn from it.
(Proverbs 22:6)

Who's in Charge of the Remote?

What values do we want to teach our children? We know we want to teach them Christian values based upon God's Word. We want those values to reflect faithfulness, servanthood, stewardship, mercy, and forgiveness. We want our children to reflect the gifts that God has given them in Baptism. What we want for our children, however, is not as simple as it once was.

We live in a post-modern world. The post-modern world believes in nothing specific but in anything the culture decides to believe. It is another form of relativism. Some of what was important to the generations before us, to our parents and grandparents, no longer seems as important in today's world. A great deal of the culture that surrounds us is influenced by what is portrayed on television. As someone quipped, does television reflect life or has life become a reflection of television? At an early age, our children are targets of one of the primary purposes of television—to not only entertain but to sell.

Television, for better and worse, can be a teacher of values as well. And as such, television teaches the values of entertainment. Everything on television, even religion and education, must pass the test of entertainment. After all, we have all been sensitized to what makes "good television."

Television continues to be the preferred form of entertainment for most families. Entertainment is not in itself sin. It is important to let entertainment be entertainment and nothing more. It's our calling as parents to bring common sense and order to television as well. We can be creative with television. Sometimes we can use it to teach or to be a short-term baby-sitter to keep our children occupied and entertained while we are busy with other things.

The concerns may be the same for all parents. How much television should a child watch each day? What limits should be placed on the types of programs a child is allowed to watch? What does television teach our children about right and wrong, parents, marriage, dating, sex, violence, religion, school, etc.? Watch one night of television and the answers are clear. This is why television is primarily entertainment.

As we struggle with these issues, we confess our own lack of total knowledge. As parents, we always remember that the gifts God gives to us and to our children in Baptism. These gifts are the foundation of our values. Sin and grace, repentence and forgiveness—these are the values that we want our children to see television with. All else is just entertainment.

But I want to watch it!

Four-year-old Kelsey loved to play with her best friend, Daria, who was six months older and ready to start kindergarten. After preschool, Kelsey would go to Daria's house and play. Lori, Kelsey's mom, liked Daria. And although she didn't know Daria's family that well, they seemed like nice people. So Lori had no concerns until the week Kelsey was home with chicken pox.

At 4:00 one afternoon, Kelsey took the television remote control and turned on a children's cartoon called "The Power Patrol." The Power Patrol was a very controversial program in which the main characters were masked crusaders who fought for truth and justice and most often did so in a very violent way.

Supporters of the program said it was like the westerns of old in which good cowboys fought against bad cowboys with their fists and with guns. They said it was a classic story of good versus evil in which the forces of good, the Power Patrol, always triumphed over the forces of evil.

Critics of the program said it did nothing more than feed into the violence spiral that society continued to experience. They also said it provided poor role models for children who watched it in that it gave children permission to express themselves violently and in very destructive ways. In fact, the critics would cite incidents of violent behavior in preschoolers that mimicked the Power Patrol program.

So as Kelsey watched the show, Lori waited patiently until the end of the program and then said, "Kelsey, I don't want you to watch that program ever again! That's terrible what those cartoon characters do to people!"

"But I have to watch it, Mommy! Daria and I are members of the Power Patrol Pack. Don't you know the Power Patrol helps people?" said Kelsey.

"You mean you've watched this program at Daria's?" Lori asked.

"Well, we watch it when Daria's mom is in another room," Kelsey replied.

"Well, I'll put an end to that!" Lori said.

What would you do?

- What might Lori have done to avoid her surprise over Kelsey's watching the Power Patrol?

- Lori's way of dealing with the incident was to let Kelsey watch the entire episode and then forbid her to watch the program again. What other way could Lori have dealt with Kelsey's desire to watch the Power Patrol?

- Kelsey's response to Lori was, "Don't you know the Power Patrol helps people?" Lori changed the subject and asked Kelsey if she had watched the program before. If you were Lori, how would you help Kelsey understand how good keeps evil under control?

• As you hear Kelsey's response that she and Daria watch the program whenever her friend's mother is not in the room, you might ask why they can't watch when her mother is in the room. What might Kelsey say?

• Lori is concerned about the violence in the cartoon. How violent was the crucifixion of Jesus? How violent is the drowning of the Old Adam in Baptism?

• Lori's final comment shuts off communication completely. Write another ending to the conversation that would give more evidence that Lori is listening to Kelsey.

• As you analyze what has happened here, take into consideration that the Power Patrol is a cartoon. Why might Kelsey take a cartoon less seriously than a live-action television program?

Who's in charge of the remote control? We might also ask, who's responsibility it is to educate our children about values and the Christian faith? If the question is asked in that light, then our answer becomes perfectly clear. Television cannot replace our role as parents. When it comes to training and educating children, parents are accountable. After all, God has called us to this role. He has called us to help our children grow emotionally, physically, and spiritually. Parents are the first and most important teachers. If we allow that call to be replaced by the media, we do a great disservice to ourselves and to our children.

As we seek answers to questions such as these and as we try to clarify our responsibility to our children in regard to watching television, it might be helpful to:

• Periodically review the programs that are offered on television and what critics say about them.

• As you evaluate the programs, think about a common sense approach to entertainment in your life and your child's life.

• Establish early in your children's life that there are times to watch television and there are times to do other things.

• Create reasonable alternatives that help family members connect with one another.

• Create a nightly or weekly family time when you play games or just talk with one another. Look for ways to include your child in family devotions by offering her the opportunity to say a prayer or sing a hymn.

• Communicate clearly at an early age to your child the programs that are acceptable and not acceptable. Don't be afraid to tell her why.

• As your child grows help him or her to understand how good needs to keep bad under control in the world.

As we try to help our children develop values and morals that express their faith in the Triune God, we can be confident that in our Baptism the Holy Spirit gave us His gifts. Those gifts are forgiveness of sins, a rescue from death and the devil, and eternal salvation. In the end, we know that our children will benefit from those gifts and that they will grow in their understanding of what it means to be a child of God.

Closing Prayer

Lord God, as I respond to the call You have given me as a parent, help me realize that although I do not have all the answers, You will give me wisdom to be the parent You would have me be. Help me always to remember the baptismal gifts you give to me and my children. In Your Son's name, I pray. Amen.

Parent Pairs

What kind of television programs should my child watch? How much television should he or she watch each day? What are the values I want my child to reflect as he or she continues to grow? What role am I willing to let television play in the selection of those values?

Read Proverbs 22:6 and consider the following questions as you discuss the **Parent Pairs** section with your spouse or with another parent.

Who's in Charge of the Remote?

(To be done with your spouse or another parent.)

1. When I was a child, I watched television more than 10 hours a week.

   Agree   Disagree

2. When I was a child, my parents never monitored my television usage.

   Agree   Disagree

3. If my parents did monitor my television usage, I was supposed to watch only certain programs; others were off limits. *(Describe both types of programs.)*

4. I believe I benefited from my parents' monitoring of my television usage.

   Agree   Disagree

5. The way I was allowed to watch television as a child affects the way I allow my child to watch television.

   Agree   Disagree

6. I believe my child's television usage should be: *(Choose one.)*
   - ❑ Limited to a certain amount of time each day.
   - ❑ Screened so my child will not be subjected to inappropriate material.
   - ❑ Limited to only educational programs.
   - ❑ Open to whatever my child wishes to watch.
   - ❑ Other.

7. A child who watches too much violence on television may become a violent child.

   Agree   Disagree

8. There is good violence and bad violence in the world.

   Agree   Disagree

9. The crucifixion of Jesus was a necessary violence.

        Agree   Disagree

10. Shows that portray the theme of good that triumphs over evil are positive shows for children to watch because they give them hope and a sense of order.

        Agree   Disagree

11. Violence and force do play a role in keeping order in the community and the world.

        Agree   Disagree

12. I have a plan that helps control the amount of time my child watches television.

        Agree   Disagree

13. My plan is:

14. The most important components of my plan are: (*Rank in order of importance with #1 being the most important, then #2, #3, etc.*)

   ___ I watch the programs that are questionable in nature with my child.

   ___ The television never becomes my baby-sitter.

   ___ The program should help my child know the difference between reality and fantasy.

   ___ I do not allow my child to watch anything that would teach values contrary to what I believe.

   ___ Recognition that television viewing is simply entertainment.

   ___ Realization that I have the right to control the remote.

   ___ Knowledge that I can write a sponsor if I object to what I see.

   ___ My ability to model my belief that no one needs to take television that seriously.

   ___ Other.

15. The strength I gain from Proverbs 22:6 is:

Thomas said to Him, "Lord, we don't know where You are going, so how can we know the way?" Jesus answered, "I am the way and the truth and the life. No one comes to the Father except through Me." (John 14:5–6)

Don't Leave Me!

It's called separation anxiety. It's often evident the first day of school or at orientation for preschool or kindergarten. It's usually more apparent in those parents who are experiencing it for the first time. First-time parents are the ones who ask about bathroom breaks, lunch lines, bus lines, what happens if their child gets lost. Separation anxiety can profoundly affect parents.

Of course, separation anxiety can also affect preschoolers. For some children, preschool is their first real transition from family and home to community and culture. Other children may have already experienced somewhat of a transition if they have been a part of a day care setting. In preschool, however, the atmosphere has changed. Somehow, young children sense that this is the beginning of something big. We know it to be the beginning of a learning curve that will continue for the rest of their lives.

Reinforced by what they know and comforted by the familiar, it is no surprise that many preschoolers experience separation anxiety when they begin school. Parents and teachers alike tell stories of children who cry for quite a while before they successfully adjust to the idea that school is a permanent change.

As parents recall anxious feelings they may have experienced as a child, they might remember wondering if, once their parents left, they would ever return. Maybe some adults remember spending worried moments at the window, gazing down the street, looking for the family car to return.

For parents, the anxiety they recall when they were children was real. The anxiety their children feel is also very real. What can parents do about their children's separation anxiety that will, in the end, equip them for situations where they must go it alone?

In the verses above, Thomas, the disciple, expressed anxiety when Jesus announced that He was going away. It was Thomas's fear that led him to say, "Lord, we do not know where You are going, so how can we know the way?" Thomas wouldn't understand until the day of Pentecost that Jesus would be with him always and forever. We can trust that the same Savior who was with Thomas remains with parents and children as they work through the anxiety of separation caused by the first day of school. It is the same Jesus who called them through His Word. It is the same Jesus who gives His body and blood in your church. That is how we know the same Jesus is with us forever. That is how we know Jesus is the way, the truth, and the life.

When are you coming back?

It was Robby Olson's first day at Shady Oak Preschool. He generally seemed to be a budding, energetic three-year-old who was confident and not worried about anything. Therefore, when his mother, Michelle, took him to preschool, she felt certain that he would have no trouble making the transition from being at home all the time to spending two days at preschool.

Michelle had no doubts—until it was time to leave Robby with his teacher, Mrs. Sweet. As she started to leave, Robby ran to his mother and hung on to her leg, crying, "Mommy, don't leave me! When are you coming back?"

Michelle calmly replied that she would be back as soon as preschool was over. When Robby pressed her, asking how long that would be, she replied, "In about two hours!"

Then Robby continued, "That's a long time! Mommy, I want you back right now!"

Plagued by a guilty conscience, Michelle persuaded Mrs. Sweet to let her stay the entire time. Michelle agreed that the next day she would leave Robby at the door. Mrs. Sweet said, "Then we'll take good care of Robby and he'll have a great time. Won't you, Robby, dear?"

The next day came and Michelle told Robby at the door, "Robby, you see there's nothing to be afraid about. Nothing will happen to you. I know you'll have a great time!"

Robby answered, "But Mommy, when are you coming back?"

Robby began to cry as he left his mom at the door and walked into the room. Two weeks later, he was still crying when Michelle picked him up after school. Before she left, Mrs. Sweet said to Michelle, "Mrs. Olson, may I talk with you for a minute?"

As they moved to a corner where Robby could see them, Mrs. Sweet said, "Mrs. Olson, you need to know that the school staff has decided that we're giving Robby one more week here. If his behavior doesn't change, I'm afraid his association with the Shady Oak Preschool will be terminated!"

As Michelle left with Robby in hand, it was her turn to cry.

What would you do?

• After reading about Robby and Michelle, we have no idea about how Michelle prepared Robby for preschool. If you were Michelle, how would you have prepared him?

• Keeping in mind that Robby's understanding of time is quite different from Michelle's, how would you have responded to Robby's question, "When are you coming back?"

• On the first day, Michelle persuades Mrs. Sweet to let her stay with Robby until the end of the preschool day. What other options do you think Michelle could have tried?

• Do you think Robby had been left with others before this? How might Sunday school help this transition?

• If you were Michelle and you heard that your child was in danger of being expelled from preschool, what would you need to hear from Mrs. Sweet? How would you respond to the teacher?

• Finally, if you were Michelle, what would you do? What choices would you make? How would you explain the choices to Robby?

In so many ways, we want our children to need us and to want us to be there for them. At the same time, we hope they develop a sense of healthy separation from us. It was necessary for Jesus to leave His disciples and separate from them. If He had not left, they would not have been able to carry on and continue His ministry. That is how Jesus gave the pastoral office to the church.

Our children need to grow as well. They need to know that they can make it on their own. They can explore new experiences and be successful in learning from them. They can apply what we teach them at home and use those skills to build meaningful relationships with pastors, teachers, and classmates. If we didn't allow this to happen, our children would never mature. In a sense, then, preschool becomes the beginning of a gift we give our children to prepare them for a world without us, and it remains a world in which their Lord and Savior, Jesus Christ, abides with them in His Word and their sacramental life.

As a result, we help our children prepare for preschool when we:

- Let them get acquainted with the building and their classroom in advance.

- Introduce them to their teachers and let their teachers know important tidbits of information about our children.

- Let our children know how excited we are about their teachers. Tell our children that their teachers love teaching preschool, and they will love teaching them.

- Be excited about this new adventure for them. Talk with them about how much fun it will be not only to meet new friends, but to learn new things as well.

- Pray for them and pray with them about the experience. Include classmates and teachers in your prayers.

- Celebrate with them when they have good days.

- Be patient and understanding when they have difficult days.

- If they have difficult days, do not be afraid to talk with your child's teacher to try to discover what, if anything, both you and your child might do differently.

As you continue to reassure your children, remind them that Jesus, who remained with Thomas, will remain with them. Let them know they are loved and they are precious in God's sight. Read Bible stories with them that show how God kept His promises to His people. And help them learn that God loves them and will keep His promises to them.

Closing Prayer

Dear God, as Your Son calmed Thomas's anxiety when he heard that Jesus was leaving, help me as a parent deal with my child's separation anxiety. Work through me to assure my child that he is loved and remains precious in Your sight and safe in Your care. In Jesus' name. Amen.

Parent Pairs

What can I do to prepare my child for a successful preschool experience? How can I deal with the situation if my child experiences anxiety?

Read John 14:5–6 and consider the following questions as you discuss the **Parent Pairs** section with your spouse or with another parent.

Don't Leave Me!

(To be done with your spouse or another parent.)

1. To minimize my child's separation anxiety, I can: *(Rank in order of importance with #1 being the most important, then #2, #3, etc.)*

___Check thoroughly with the preschool about its philosophy and its teachers. As a part of that check, I will ask the teachers how they set limits and show support and affection.

___Show my excitement about the preschool adventure, and share my excitement with my child.

___Thoroughly prepare my child by letting her see the room, meet the teacher, and even practice making a few dry runs to school.

___Allow my child to express her fears.

___Help my child remember other times when I have left her and have come back, like at Sunday school.

___Not worry about separation anxiety because I know it is part of growing up.

___Other.

2. The most important thing I can do for my child as I take him to preschool is: *(Choose one.)*

❑ Pray that the experience will be a rewarding one for my child and for me.

❑ Share only my excitement and assure my child that everything will be all right.

❑ Stay silent because I'm not sure what I could say that would help him.

❑ Be aware of feelings and be ready to accept them as valid, no matter what they might be.

❑ Other.

3. Two people I would talk with if my child were experiencing anxiety about preschool, would be:

4. I would want these people to help me by:

5. Three ways I have dealt with separation anxiety in the past that were helpful have been:

6. Two ways that were not helpful were:

7. One plan I have to deal with separation anxiety in the future is:

8. My greatest anxiety as I separate from my child as our preschool experience begins is:

9. I can best deal with my own anxiety by:

10. My prayer for my child and her teachers as she goes to preschool is:

11. The strength I gain from John 14:5–6 is:

Abraham looked up and there in a thicket he saw a ram caught by its horns. He went over and took the ram and sacrificed it as a burnt offering instead of his son. So Abraham called that place The LORD Will Provide. And to this day it is said, "On the mountain of the LORD it will be provided." (Genesis 22:13–14)

Who'll Be My Daddy?

Who will take care of me? Whether preschoolers realize it, that is perhaps the most basic question they ask each and every day. The question takes shape when they get up in the morning and wonder what they will wear. It manifests itself when they come to the breakfast table and wonder what they will eat. It stays with them as they go to day care or preschool. The answer for most preschoolers is very clear. In two-parent homes, mommy and daddy provide for them. In the single parent home, the continuum of care is provided by the single parent.

Questions are inevitable when a transition occurs in the lives of these precious young people, especially when that transition involves the changes that come with divorce. Then the question "Who will take care of me?" looms large on the horizon of their world. "Where will I live? Who will I live with? Who are these new people in my life? How often will I see Mommy or Daddy? Will I be able to see my friends?" All of these questions revolve around the central theme of someone they can count on to provide for them. They want to be assured that there will be a continuum of care from the people they love and trust.

Although the story is dramatic in nature and reflects an event in the life of Abraham and Isaac, similar questions may have occurred to this father and son. A clash of our reason and God's Word is apparent. How could God ask Abraham to sacrifice his son? We don't have to make sense out of God's Word, we believe and trust in God above all things. As Abraham was about to sacrifice his only son, God provided. God provided a ram and Isaac's life was spared. Years later, another father, our heavenly Father, sacrificed His only Son so we might be spared and so we can be assured that God always provides for our eternal life as well as our daily life.

God provides for children through parents. God provides, although divorce may be worse than death for the parents who are involved. God provides, even when children become innocent victims of a power struggle between parents or grandparents. God provides, even in the midst of the fear, grief, or separation anxiety. God provides and assures the preschooler that although the relationship between his parents has failed, the relationship he has with his mother and with his father will continue. Most important, the relationship he has with his heavenly Father will never fail because Jesus has made it so! God's Son, Jesus, kept His promise to die on the cross for our sin. Jesus provides the mercy, strength, and forgiveness that parents and children need.

I'll still be your daddy!

Rick and Sandy had been married for six years. During that time, they had one child, Kari, who had just turned four years old. Kari was the apple of her father's eye. Whenever he was home, Rick played games with her, read books to her, and took walks with her. Kari, in turn, loved her daddy very much.

Although Rick and Kari had a good relationship, he and Sandy did not. They fought constantly. After they married, they realized that the vast differences in their backgrounds surfaced in the way they related to each other. Rick came from a home where his father had been an alcoholic and his mother supported the family by working two jobs. Sandy came from a family that was alcohol-free, a family in which her parents communicated very well with each other and did many things together. Sandy's was the family Rick never experienced but always wanted.

After months of counseling, Rick and Sandy came to the decision that they would divorce. They knew the most difficult part would be telling Kari.

One evening after supper, they sat with Kari to tell her. Sandy began, "Kari, your daddy and I have something to tell you. You know that your daddy and I love you very much. You are so important to both of us. What we're telling you is that your daddy and I are getting a divorce. Do you know what that means?"

"I think so!" Kari said, fighting back the tears. "Jimmy's mom and dad got a divorce and Jimmy never sees his daddy. Jimmy's mom married another man and he has a new daddy! Does that mean I'm getting a new daddy? I don't want a new daddy! I want my daddy!"

It was Rick's turn. "Kari, I'll always be your daddy! Kari, I haven't stopped loving you! I just won't be living in the same house with you and your mom. You know that Mommy and I argue a lot. We just finally decided that we can't do that to each other anymore. It's hurting us, and we're afraid it's hurting you!"

"But when will I see you? " Kari asked.

Rick told her, "You'll see me every other weekend and probably one day during the week. Then, when summer comes, you'll probably see me a lot more than you do even now!"

"I don't want you to leave, Daddy!" Kari cried.

What would you do?

- Attempt for a moment to imagine that you are Kari and try to describe what she might be feeling. What might be her greatest fears?

- Sandy began the discussion. On what basis do you think it was decided that Sandy should begin? How might the discussion have been different if Rick began the talk with Kari?

- Sandy ends her introduction of the news of the divorce by asking Kari if she knows what divorce means. What more might Sandy have said to ease

Kari's anxiety rather than asking her that question?

• Rick decides to answer Kari's question about getting a new daddy by reassuring her that he will always be her daddy. How else might Rick have answered Kari's question?

• God gives two reasons for divorce: desertion and infidelity. How can Rick and Sandy prepare Kari for this? Where does repentence and forgiveness come in?

• When Kari asks Rick if she will see him anymore, he is very specific and says exactly when she will see him. How is Rick's explanation helpful for Kari? How might it be not that helpful?

• Let's turn the discussion around and say that it is Sandy who is leaving the home and Rick who becomes the primary custodial parent. How might the entire story have changed?

• What else could Rick and Sandy say to assure Kari that they will continue to provide for her and that God will continue to provide for her?

Divorce results in pain and heartache for many. It is not only the children of divorcing parents who ask, "Who will provide for us?" Parents may ask that question as they face the reality that their household income will change. Both the husband and the wife will need emotional support. At one time or another, both may feel abandoned and alone. Both will need to struggle with God's Word and see where their sin came into the decision. God brings healing and peace to such a parent for He Himself suffered in pain and torture—even paid for these sins in a broken marriage.

Yet in the midst of the myriad feelings they experience, they still are called to be parents and to provide for their children. In addition, they still try to help their children come to grips with their actions even when it is impossible for their children to completely comprehend why they are ending the marriage. A significant challenge for divorcing parents is to remain focused on the needs of their children. As they concentrate on those needs, preferably the divorcing parents treat each other with kindness and respect. Once again, the matter of provision should take center stage as the divorcing parents ask, "How can we best parent our children when we no longer are married?"

In a situation that is filled with grief and loss, anxiety and uncertainty, it is important for both mother and father to constantly reinforce that they love their son or daughter. It is especially important that parents are clear with their children that their divorce was not caused by something the child did or did not do. All too often, children live with the misguided belief that they were the cause of their parents' divorce, that if only they had been better children, better behaved, the divorce would not have happened. Many children also fantasize that someday their parents will come back together and that they will live happily ever after as one family. For the sake of the children, divorcing parents can help their children with these issues and let them know clearly that despite the end of the marriage, their relationship with their children will continue.

Although divorce was never a part of God's plan, or the plan of most parents for that matter, we need to let our children know that God loves and forgives. He continues to provide for the divorcing parents and also for the children. Unfortunately, the brokeness of divorce provides an opportunity for children to learn about the difference between the call to be a parent and the call to be a spouse. May we pray that families that experience divorce are reassured by that continuing provision of God's everlasting grace.

Closing Prayer

O God, as you spared Abraham the sacrifice of Isaac, help divorcing parents work through their own pain and strive to spare their sons and daughters needless pain and heartache. Provide for the children patience and kindness so they might know that the relationship with their parents will continue and their relationship with You will never fail. In Jesus' name I pray. Amen.

Parent Pairs

How can parents who are divorcing share that news with their children and, at the same time, reassure them of their love? What can parents do to lessen their children's anxiety throughout the divorce process? How can parents let their children know that in the midst of a divorce they—and God—will continue to love them and provide for them?

Read Genesis 22:13–14 and consider the following questions as you discuss the **Parent Pairs** section with your spouse or with another parent.

Who'll Be My Daddy?

(To be done with your spouse or another parent.)

1. I grew up with parents who divorced.

> Agree   Disagree

2. When I was a child, the children I knew who came from divorced homes had a great deal of difficulty adjusting to the divorce.

> Agree   Disagree

3. I believe that: *(You may choose more than one answer.)*
   - ❏ Divorce is sinful and not what God intended.
   - ❏ Divorce is unfortunate but can be a tragic necessity.
   - ❏ Divorce is always harmful for children.
   - ❏ Divorcing parents can use the experience to teach their children how to continue to relate to someone even after the relationship has ended.
   - ❏ Divorce teaches children great survival skills.
   - ❏ Other.

4. Children need to be told the truth in the case of a divorce, even if the truth means telling about one partner's unfaithfulness.

> Agree   Disagree

5. A divorced parent needs to reassure his children that he will continue to provide for them, by:

6. Divorced parents need to reassure their children that God will continue to provide for them, by:

7. I believe it is perfectly all right to use as one of the reasons for divorce that Mom and Dad staying together would be harmful for the children.

               Agree   Disagree

8. Divorced parents main concern should be: *(Rank in order of importance, with #1 being the most important, then #2, #3, etc.)*

    ___That they are fair in their treatment of each other and what is said about each other.

    ___That the children be assured of the consistency of their love.

    ___That the children know they are not to blame for their divorce.

    ___That the other spouse is fairly treated and does not speak badly about the other to the children.

    ___That the spouse is consistent in his financial support of the children.

    ___That the divorced person waits at least a year to be involved in another relationship.

    ___That the spouse is able to show her children that she is able to get on with her life without her spouse.

    ___That he makes each time he see his children quality time.

    ___That divorced parents are able to support each other in their attempts to parent their children.

    ___That the divorced parents are able to take care of their children in a way that does not threaten them or do emotional or spiritual damage to them.

    ___Other.

9. The strength I gain from Genesis 22:13–14 is:

We were therefore buried with Him through baptism into death in order that, just as Christ was raised from the dead through the glory of the Father, we too may live a new life. (Romans 6:4)

When Grandpa Dies . . .

Since the fall of Adam and Eve into sin, death has been a part of life. In the early years of our country, death took place in the midst of a caring, loving family and usually occurred in the home. In recent decades, we have gradually removed death from the midst of our lives. More often than not, people die in hospitals or in nursing homes, not at home. Visitations and the viewing of the deceased loved one no longer take place in homes, they take place in funeral chapels where the sting of death is not as apparent. Large backlit rooms provide a place where we can pay our final respects to our loved ones and offer condolences to the grieving in a pleasant surrounding. While cards, flowers, and casseroles may fill our homes, the deceased is not there.

As we have removed death from the middle of everyday life, we might wonder what we want to teach our children about death and how we want them to react. Because many parents themselves might be uncomfortable with death, they are also uncomfortable attempting to help their children deal with it. But that doesn't detract from what was true at the beginning of time—death is a part of life as a result of our fallen creation.

As Christians we have something very important about death to share with our children. Death is not the final word. Satan does not triumph in the life of a believer or in the death of a believer. Sometimes we forget why Baptism is so important at a funeral—it is the theme of every Christian's life. Baptisms and funerals both celebrate the victory over sin and death that Jesus earned for us and gave to us. We can confidently share this truth and this hope with our children regardless of their age.

With this truth in mind, we have a great opportunity to teach our children about heaven. We can acknowledge that the God who is with our departed loved one throughout eternity remains with us. Our child's entire life is a sacramental life. God comes to us and calls us to Him in Baptism and the Lord's Supper. We prepare our children most of their young lives to participate in the presence of Christ at this Holy Meal. There, Jesus brings together—to be one in Him—all of the saints in heaven and on earth. We can help our children embrace their Savior and trust that even in death, He offers all who believe a new beginning and eternal life with Him.

I don't want her there!

Sherry was in a state of shock. She had learned only 24 hours before that her dad had died suddenly of a heart attack. She still couldn't believe it. He was only 62 and had talked about retiring in a year or two and then traveling with her mother.

Now she sat in her parents' living room. She sat in the same chair her dad had always sat in while he smoked his pipe, read the paper, or watched football. Her husband, Bob, and her mother, Evelyn, were also in the room. It was Evelyn who spoke first.

"You know, Sherry, I don't think Lindsey should go to the funeral. After all, she's only four and she won't understand what is happening. Or if you let her go to the funeral, I really don't think she should go to the visitation."

Sherry bolted upright. She hadn't given much thought to Lindsey; she had been so consumed with her own grief. In fact, it was Bob who had told Lindsey about her grandfather. All Sherry could do was cry. As her mother spoke, she admitted that she didn't know what to do. She wanted Lindsey with her, but she was afraid that she would be too consumed with grief to be an attentive mother.

Sherry said, "I guess you're right, Mother. Maybe it's better for Lindsey if she doesn't attend. I don't want her lasting memory of her grandfather to be of him lying in a coffin." She swallowed hard on her last words as tears began to fall heavily again.

Bob took his turn. "You know, I disagree with both of you. Ever since I told Lindsey that grandpa died, she keeps saying to me, 'Where is he? Is he coming back? Why can't I see him?' Both of you know how attached she was to her grandpa and how much she loved him. I think she should go to the funeral home to say good-bye to grandpa and she should go to the funeral as well. What better way is there to learn about death than at the funeral of her beloved grandfather!"

Sherry looked at her mother and then looked at Bob as she said, "Bob, it's not right! I don't want her there!"

What would you do?

- Sherry's mother states that since Lindsey is only four, she won't understand and she shouldn't go to the funeral. What do you think is important for Lindsey to understand? Should her ability to understand determine whether she goes to the funeral?

- After Sherry cuts through her shock and confusion, she states, "I don't want Lindsey's lasting memory of her grandfather to be of him lying in a coffin." If you were trying to defend her statement, what would you say to support her point of view?

- At this point, Bob enters the conversation and shares Lindsey's questions: "Where is he? Is he coming back? Why can't I see him?" If you were Bob or Sherry, how would you respond?

- Bob states that the purpose of the funeral would be to help Lindsey say good-bye and help her begin to understand more about death. As you think about your faith, what other functions of a funeral could you identify?

- Sherry's way of handling the situation is to say with finality, "I don't want her there!" If you were Bob, what would you say next and why would you say it?

- If you were a friend of Sherry or Bob, what would you recommend, and why?

- In the end, what are the reasons Lindsey should go to the funeral? What are the reasons Lindsey should not attend?

Death is a part of life as a result of our fall into sin. The sooner we teach our children that fact, the sooner they grasp the comfort of the resurrection God gave to them. The more we invite our children to join us in the process of grieving the loss of a loved one, the more we can do to lessen their anxiety. The day will come when they realize that death not only happens to grandpas and grandmas, but death happens to mothers and fathers, sisters and brothers. Death ultimately will happen to them. But at each step they will learn more about Christ's gifts of forgiveness and resurrection.

Until that day comes, however, we as parents can help our children deal with death by:

- *Not being afraid to talk about death and answer questions they have.* Remember that sometimes children who ask questions aren't asking us to give them all the information we know, they're usually asking for specific details. Questions like "where are grandpa's legs?" are simply put and simply answered. Our children want to see the other half of the coffin.

- *Allowing them to be sad and to see that we are sad.* Grieving causes tears to flow. Just because we cry does not mean that we don't believe that a loved one is rejoicing in heaven.

- *Allowing them to find their own ways to say good-bye.* Placing pictures of themselves or pictures they have drawn in the coffins of their loved ones comforts some children. It is their way to express their grief and also it is a way to say a personal good-bye.

- *Preparing our children beforehand.* Helping them understand what they will see and experience before they enter a funeral chapel, participate in a service, or travel to the cemetery will satisfy curiosity and help lessen anxiety about the emotions they may see expressed.

- *Rely on available resources.* Ask your pastor or a librarian for age-appropriate Christian books that reflect our faith and our hope in the resurrection of eternal life for all who believe in Jesus as our risen Savior.

- *Trust the Lord's power in their lives.* Children's faith is simple, not because it is different than parent's faith. God's Word is simply believed by them! Parents are often surprised by how quickly children move through grief.

As we teach our children about death, may we remember what Paul said in his letter to the Romans—that Christians have already died and risen in the Lord in Baptism. Remind them that one day they too will rejoice with all the saints in heaven. Jesus prepares us for the resurrection on the Last Day when there will be a great reunion where we will celebrate with our loved ones forever!

Closing Prayer

Loving Savior, You are compassionate and kind. You defeated death on the cross for me. As I mourn the loss of people I love, treat me with compassion and kindness. Give me strength that I might witness to my children that the eternal life You give is a life that not even death can destroy. In Your victorious name, I pray. Amen.

Parent Pairs

How can I help my preschooler understand when someone they love dies? How can my preschooler participate in the grieving process in ways that are age appropriate? What do I want my child to learn about death and about the hope of the resurrection that God gives us in His Son, Jesus Christ?

Read Romans 6:4 and consider the following questions as you discuss the **Parent Pairs** section with your spouse or with another parent.

When Grandpa Dies . . .

(To be done with your spouse or another parent.)

1. My earliest memory of attending a funeral was when I was _____. *(Fill in your age.)*

2. Describe what that funeral was like for you:

3. When I was a child, my parents talked openly about death.

   Agree   Disagree

4. When I was a child, the thought of death frightened me.

   Agree   Disagree

5. My childhood experience with death greatly influences how I teach my children about death.

   Agree   Disagree

6. I think children under four years old do not need to attend a funeral.

   Agree   Disagree

7. The most important aspect of a funeral for a young child is: *(Rank in order of importance with #1 being the most important, then #2, #3, etc.)*

   ____That it allows them a chance to view the body.

   ____That it helps them say good-bye to their loved one.

   ____That it enables them to learn more about death.

   ____That it is an opportunity for them to hear that Jesus has triumphed over death.

   ____That it allows them to participate in the grieving process.

   ____That it helps them say in their own way how important their loved one was in their life.

   ____That it helps them deal with questions they might have about where their loved one is or what has happened to their loved one.

   ____That it helps me teach them about the gifts God gave them in Baptism.

   ____Other.

8. My prayer for my child as he or she faces the death of a loved one would be:

9. My prayer for me as I help my child face the death of a loved one would be:

10. If I died before my child was three or four, I would want my child to attend my funeral.

   Agree   Disagree

11. If I died before my child was three or four, I would want my child to view my dead body.

   Agree   Disagree

12. I think funerals help children deal with the reality of death.

   Agree   Disagree

13. If I died before my child was three or four, I would hope my spouse or relatives would share these three important things about me:

14. When I die, I hope this epitaph will appear on my tombstone:

15. When I die, I really don't care how my loved ones dispose of my remains.

     Agree   Disagree

16. The strength I gain from Romans 6:4 is:

Observe the Sabbath day by keeping it holy…For you are a holy people to the LORD your God. The LORD your God has chosen you, to be His people, His treasured possession.
(Deuteronomy 5:12; 7:6)

When Sunday Comes

Since the beginning of creation, God established the Sabbath for His people to receive His gifts of mercy, rest, worship, and to give back to Him what He has given to them. In Old Testament times, the Sabbath practice was to worship on Saturday, the seventh day of the week. God's people worshiped on Saturday because He rested on the seventh day after He finished the work of creation.

That Sabbath practice was changed from Saturday to Sunday after Jesus' resurrection on the first Easter. New Testament Christians wanted their Sabbath observance to celebrate the day Jesus rose victorious from the dead. They observed every Sabbath day as a reminder to all who worshiped Jesus that He defeated death, sin, and the power of Satan by His suffering, death, and resurrection.

Thousands of years later, Sunday remains our primary day of worship. Sundays are when Christ calls His people together as the body of Christ to hear His Word and receive the gifts of the sacraments. As we come together as the church, we are refreshed and renewed because we are made holy through forgiveness. We can only respond with praise and thanksgiving to our God.

The last thing we want our worship experience to be is energy draining. Unfortunately, for parents with young children, that's exactly what it can be. Many families who attempt to sit quietly in church with their toddlers or preschoolers spend more time trying to pacify their children than participating in worship. In fact, many mothers or fathers find that they spend more time in the halls, cry rooms, or restrooms than they do in the sanctuary. However, training our children from birth to hear the baptismal call from Christ is the most important thing a Christian parent will do. After your child is baptized, preparing for Christ's Holy Meal is the focus of their lives.

If it were only the families of those active children who were affected, perhaps the parents could be persistent and patient enough to go with the flow, so to speak, and remain in the sanctuary during the service. Unfortunately, many parents of young children have felt the cold stares of other parishioners whose worship has been disturbed by these little ones.

How do parents begin to incorporate their children into the corporate worship experience? What are the goals of parents as they bring their children to services? As we ask such questions, we might remember that all who believe and are baptized into Christ, young and old, are a valued part of Christ's body. As such, Christ welcomes everyone to worship. Helping young children learn how to participate in church and how to behave so others may participate is an ongoing challenge. But with patience and diligence, we can teach our little ones how.

What are we going to do?

It was Kris and Karl's first Sunday at a new church. They had moved from a large community to a smaller town where Karl had just been hired as a business administrator for a large local business. Kris and Karl were excited as they brought their two-year-old son, Steven, with them to the worship service.

When they walked into the church, they looked for a nursery for Steven, but when they saw it, they hesitated. A 13-year-old girl staffed it. Already, there were eight children playing. Kris looked at Karl. Karl looked at Kris. Finally Kris said, "Karl, at least for this first time, let's take Steven with us to church."

Kris thought: *Won't this be nice. We'll be in church for the first time as a family.* At their previous congregation, Steven went to the nursery every Sunday. Their church also had a special children's time, which meant that the children were invited forward for a children's message, and then those who were of Sunday school age left the service for Sunday school. As a result, their worship service in their former church was usually without interruption from any children whose attention span didn't allow them to sit through a service without activity.

Before the service began, Kris and Karl slipped into the last pew and waited patiently. Halfway through the service, Steven began to fidget. He spent time on the floor under the pew. He looked around at the people next to him and behind him. Then, as he was climbing onto the pew from the floor, he slipped and hit his head on the pew in front of him. He let out a screech and the tears began to flow. Frustrated, worried, and a little out of sorts, Kris gathered him up and carried him out into the hallway. As she did, she felt as if the eyes of the entire congregation were fixed only on her.

After the service was over, the pastor greeted them and said, "I'm glad you were here this Sunday, I hope I see you again!" Kris and Karl politely thanked the pastor, and as they left the church, Kris breathed a sigh of relief and said, "Am I glad that's over!"

What would you do?

- It appears as though Steven had never been to church before. If Kris and Karl had taken the time, how might they have prepared Steven for his first church service?

- What did Karl and Kris need so they would be assured that their child would be welcomed in this new church? What signals might let them know that children were welcome in the service?

- When Karl and Kris went to the nursery, they saw that a 13-year-old staffed it. For them, that raised questions about the reliability of this nursery experience. If you were Karl and Kris, what assurances would you need to make you feel comfortable about leaving Steven in the nursery?

- Karl and Kris sit in the back of the sanctuary. If you were Karl and Kris, what other options for seating would you consider? Why might you consider other options?

- When Steven is in the pew during the service, it appears as if he is allowed to do anything he pleases. How might Karl and Kris be more effective at establishing limits for Steven? What would those limits accomplish?

- It also appears as if Karl and Kris begin the worship service with nothing to help Steven occupy his time. If they were better prepared, how might they help Steven cope with his short attention span?

Worship is when the Lord comes to us in the proclaiming of His Word and in the sacraments of Holy Baptism and Holy Communion. For participants, worship is a time of confession and absolution, prayer and celebration, a time for praise, reflection, and joy. If we as parents become so busy trying to keep our children quiet, we are tempted to think that we will get absolutely nothing from being at church. In fact, we might become so frustrated that we leave the service feeling drained and exhausted.

To better equip our children to be part of the worship experience, consider the following:

- *Create a worship time at home.* Set aside time each day to read a Bible story or devotion, say prayers, and sing hymns. Children will sit more quietly in worship if they have been expected to sit quietly while Mom or Dad reads a Bible story to them.

- *Make sure your children know what church is.* Remind them that church is where Jesus is present to forgive them in person! All of the saints are gathered at the throne of God in church.

- *Prepare your children for their experience.* Tell them things like, "We are in God's house, and when we are in God's house, these are the things we do … these are the things we don't do. …"

- *Teach your children the biblical language of the church.* As you and your children sit in church, don't forget that as they slowly learn the liturgy, or the language of the church, they are also learning the biblical teachings of Christ. These will be imprinted on their soul, mind, and tongue for the rest of their lives.

- *Bring things along to occupy them when their attention span runs out.* Christian coloring books and children's bulletin inserts teach more than you think. Not only will they help your child's attention span, your child will also learn about the stories of the Bible through these specially designed materials.

- *Sit where your child can see what is happening.* Know that if a child cannot see what is happening, he more than likely will become disinterested in the worship service.

- *Be patient yet respectful of what other people need in the worship service.* Realize that your child will not be perfect and sit as long as you would want him to sit. Be respectful of other parishioners' needs to hear God's Word and be in His presence at the altar.

All believers are members of the body of Christ: young and old alike. The challenge as well as the opportunity for parents is to help their young children be aware of what it means to be a member of that wonderful body. The best way to help children be aware of their membership in Christ's church is through worship. At the same time, it truly is incumbent upon and important for congregations to do what they can to be a child-friendly, welcoming congregation. With congregations and parents working together, worship will be what God says it is: All the saints gathered in the presence of the Victorious Lamb where He gives out His merciful and forgiving gifts.

Closing Prayer

O Lord God, I love to worship You and sing Your praises. I need to receive your grace through Your Word and Sacrament. Help me to teach my child to embrace that same passion for worshiping You. Help my child learn that as a member of the body of Christ, it is a joy and privilege to receive the gifts of Your Word and to praise Your holy name. Amen.

Parent Pairs

When is a child ready to worship with his or her parents? What are parents' long-range objectives for their children when they bring them to worship? How long should a parent stay in a service when their child's attention span has lapsed? How can parents prepare their children for worship so they and their children will be refreshed and renewed by their experience?

Read Deuteronomy 5:12 and 7:6 and consider the following questions as you discuss the **Parent Pairs** section with your spouse or with another parent.

When Sunday Comes

(To be done with your spouse or another parent.)

1. When I was a young child, I attended church regularly.

   Agree   Disagree

2. If I acted out in church, my parents: *(Choose one.)*
   - ☐ Immediately took me out of the service.
   - ☐ Said nothing but I would hear about it when we got home.
   - ☐ Tried to distract me with other things.
   - ☐ Gave me one warning and then took me out of the service.
   - ☐ Other.

3. My church attendance, or my lack of church attendance, when I was a child affects my views on my children attending church.

   Agree   Disagree

4. The church we attend is child friendly.

   Agree   Disagree

5. To help my child understand that she is holy and that we are in the presence of God I need to do these three things:

6. I believe children should remain in church no matter how they act.

   Agree   Disagree

7. I think the main task of parents as they bring their children to church is: *(Rank in order of importance with #1 being the most important, then #2, #3, etc.)*
   - ___To make sure their children are quiet and respectful.
   - ___To prepare their children for the experience of worship.
   - ___To bring materials with them to help their children keep busy in worship.
   - ___To include their children in the worship service by continuing to explain what is taking place.
   - ___To drop their children off in the nursery so they won't disturb adults.
   - ___Other.

8. I believe our church's worship services would be more child friendly if they: (*You may choose more than one.*)

❑ Provided activity bags for young children with crayons and pictures for them to color during the service.

❑ Provided a special place for young children to sit with their families so they may see what is happening during the service.

❑ Provided a cry room near the sanctuary where moms and dads can take their child yet remain connected to the service.

❑ Educated the congregation about the importance of everyone worshiping as a family, regardless of age.

❑ Other.

9. I have family devotions with my children regularly.

Agree   Disagree

10. My ultimate goal for my children when I bring them to worship is:

11. When I attend worship with my children, I want to make sure that I receive from the experience:

12. The strength I receive from Deuteronomy 5:12 and 7:6 is: